PROPHETIC ACTIVATIONS

101 Exercises to Activate and Sharpen Your Prophetic Voice

Volume 1

Jennifer LeClaire

Best-Selling Author of *The Making of a Prophet*

DEDICATION

This book is dedicated to the elders who have gone before me to pioneer the modern-day prophetic movement, in particular my spiritual father, Bishop Bill Hamon. He paid a high price to see the restoration of prophets and prophetic ministry with appropriate biblical guidelines.

Should Jesus tarry, Bishop's work will continue to equip generations of prophets who seek to prepare the way for the Lord's return.

I also want to acknowledge the pioneering work of Cindy Jacobs in healing nations, James Goll in the realm of the seer anointing, and Dr. Sharon Stone, who helped pioneer the movement in Asia and the United Kingdom. Indeed, there are too many to name here. I am grateful for the relationships and the influence these elders have had on my life.

INTRODUCTION

God is speaking more than we are listening. In this hour, He is giving fresh revelation to a new generation of prophetic believers, yet many struggle to discern His voice amid worldly chatter and demonic distractions. If we are not walking in consistent revelation, we must conclude that the problem is on our end. Indeed, God is broadcasting, but we are not always receiving the Holy Spirit's communication.

The answer to this problem is clear: We must exercise and sharpen our spiritual senses. Hebrews 5:14 describes the spiritually mature, whose senses are trained by practice. We practice by spending more time getting to know Him, His ways, and His voice through any communication channel He uses.

If we want to truly step into the prophetic dimension God is calling us to, we must move beyond passivity and embrace intentionality. The Bible tells us to "earnestly desire spiritual gifts, especially that you may prophesy" (1 Corinthians 14:1). That word "desire" speaks of an active pursuit. It's not enough to want the gift—we must develop it through practice, obedience, and alignment with the Holy Spirit.

This is why I wrote *Prophetic Activations: 101 Exercises to Activate and Sharpen Your Prophetic Voice*. I long to see a generation rise with boldness, precision, and clarity in their prophetic utterances. I want you to recognize that hearing from God is not just for a select few but for anyone who chooses to cultivate intimacy with the Father and operate by faith. You were created to hear God's voice and have the capacity to speak forth His Word with accuracy and authority to those to whom He sends you.

These exercises are designed to stretch you, challenge you, and pull you out of your comfort zone. Some may seem simple, and others may stretch you in unexpected ways. However, each activation is rooted in biblical principles that will help you grow in your ability to discern God's voice and share His heart with those around you.

Let this be your season to go deeper. Don't settle for secondhand revelation or a dull prophetic edge. Whether you are just beginning to use this gift or have been operating in it for years, this book will help you fine-tune your spiritual ears and sharpen your prophetic voice.

Let's partner with the Holy Spirit to amplify God's voice on earth and release His plans and purposes into the lives of those we are called to serve. It's time to exercise your spiritual gifts, sharpen your voice, and hear God like never before.

Check out Jennifer LeClaire's School of the Spirit (www.schoolofthespirit.tv), where I offer training for prophets and prophetic people.

Now, let's begin.

HOW TO USE THIS BOOK

I compiled many of these prophetic activations while teaching students worldwide about the prophetic anointing—both in live settings and through my online School of the Prophecy and Elijah Company intensives (*www.schoolofthespirit.tv*).

These exercises have been tested as part of my prophetic training curriculum, designed to stretch and sharpen your spiritual senses. Many of them were further refined through prophetic drills I developed for members of the Ignite Network (*www.jenniferleclaire.org/ignite*) where believers are equipped to step into their prophetic destinies with boldness and precision.

You can start on any page in *Prophetic Activations*, but I highly recommend beginning with the introduction and the foundational chapters on impartation and activation. These early chapters are designed to lay a solid foundation for operating in the prophetic while staying grounded in Scripture and avoiding error. As you move through the book chapter by chapter, page by page, the exercises will begin to build your faith, sharpen your discernment, and stretch your prophetic voice in ways you may never have imagined.

The entry-level activations are designed to be simple and practical, helping you gain early momentum and build confidence. Success breeds confidence, and confidence paves the way for boldness. After reading the entire book, you'll be prepared to revisit the activations that resonated with you the most or even explore new exercises as you grow in the prophetic.

I encourage you to practice these activations in various settings. Spend time with the Holy Spirit, tuning your spiritual ears to His voice. Prophesy to yourself—even if it feels awkward at first. Look into the mirror and release the Word of the Lord over your life. Declare what God is saying about your destiny, your purpose, and your future. This is a safe way to practice if you're not quite ready to prophesy over others.

But at some point, you need to take a step of faith. God has not given us a spirit of fear but of power, love, and a sound mind (2 Timothy 1:7). Step into the community of believers—the company of prophets. There is a unique corporate anointing that can amplify your gift when you prophesy in a group setting. Practicing these exercises with trusted friends or mentors not only strengthens your confidence but also provides the accountability and feedback you need to sharpen your accuracy.

Remember, this is a journey, not a sprint. God is faithful to meet you where you are as you lean into His Spirit. With every exercise, you are stepping closer to the fullness of what He has called you to in the prophetic. So, press in, keep practicing, and watch God use you to speak forth His heart with clarity, boldness, and precision.

Now, let's get started. Your voice matters in the Kingdom.

TABLE OF CONTENTS

CHAPTER 1

Understanding Impartation

Impartation is indeed a powerful and scriptural concept, carrying the weight of heaven's authority and the promise of supernatural empowerment. It is not merely a religious act or tradition; rather, it is a divine transfer—an exchange between the Spirit of God and His people, releasing an ability, an anointing, or a grace that was not previously present. Impartation cannot be learned or earned; it must be received by faith. This truth underscores the profound nature of impartation as an act of God's sovereign will and generosity.

The ministry of impartation is foundational to the New Testament Church. Paul, in his letter to the Romans, expressed a deep desire to impart spiritual gifts: "For I long to see you, that I may impart to you some spiritual gift, so that you may be strengthened. This is so that I may be encouraged together with you by each other's faith, both yours and mine" (Romans 1:11-12). Here, the Greek word for "impart" signifies a giving, a sharing, or a transfer.

Impartation can come directly from God or through anointed men and women of faith who convey what God wants you to receive. God's storehouse of gifts is limitless, and He often chooses to distribute those gifts through His anointed vessels. The laying on of hands is a key biblical method of impartation. We see this modeled repeatedly in Scripture, whether it is Moses imparting the spirit to the seventy elders (see Numbers 11:24-25) or Paul's ministry to Timothy. These acts were not just symbolic; they were spiritual transactions that empowered individuals to step into divine assignments.

Impartation Through Revelation

While the laying on of hands is one method of impartation, we must never limit God. Impartation can also occur through hearing the Word in a Spirit-charged atmosphere. When the Word is preached under the anointing, it can unlock revelation, release faith, and activate dormant gifts within the listener. This is why it's so critical to position ourselves in atmospheres where the Spirit of God is moving freely. Scripture reveals at least five areas where impartation is evident:

1. Blessings: Jacob received a blessing from Isaac that shaped his destiny (see Genesis 28:1-4).
2. Baptism in the Holy Spirit: The laying on of hands by the apostles saw people filled with the Spirit of God (see Acts 8:14-20).
3. Spiritual Gifts: Gifts were imparted through prophecy and the laying on of hands (see 1 Timothy 4:14).
4. Service: The seven chosen men were set apart for service by the laying on of hands (see Acts 6:1-8).
5. Healing Ministry: Jesus imparted authority to His disciples to heal the sick and cast out demons (see Mark 7:27).

The reality of impartation is this: it empowers you to do what you could not do in your own strength. Whether it's stepping into a new level of ministry, receiving boldness to preach the Gospel, or operating in the gifts of the Spirit, impartation is God's way of equipping His people for His purposes.

I believe you will receive an impartation of faith and prophetic anointing by reading this book. Approach this divine exchange with reverence and faith, knowing that God is eager to pour out His Spirit upon all who are willing to receive.

CHAPTER 2

Embracing Activation

You may already possess spiritual gifts within you—gifts that God has deposited for a divine purpose—but they may be lying dormant, untapped, and unused. Why? Often, it's due to a lack of awareness of the gifts themselves or a lack of understanding about how to operate in those gifts. You can't steward what you don't recognize, and you can't fully function in what you don't activate.

This is where activation becomes critical. The word "activate," in this context, carries the weight of preparation and commission. It means "to set up or formally institute (as a military unit) with the necessary personnel and equipment; to put an individual or unit on active duty." It's not a casual concept—it's a call to action. It's a charge to move from potential to purpose, from theory to practice, and from gifting to operation.

Ultimately, impartation may come through God or the laying on of hands, but activation comes from a divine charge—a commissioning into Kingdom service. Jesus modeled this when He activated the disciples in their impartation with this powerful command: "As you go, preach, saying, 'The kingdom of heaven is at hand.' Heal the sick, cleanse the lepers, raise the dead, and cast out demons" (Matthew 10:7-8).

Notice the progression. The disciples didn't just receive an impartation to sit on; they were immediately charged to act. They were given a clear mandate, a mission that required them to step out in faith, trust the anointing, and exercise their spiritual authority.

When the Lord gives you a gift, He expects you to use it. Gifts are not ornamental; they are functional. They are given to glorify God, edify the Church, and advance His kingdom. Just as you receive impartation by faith, you must also take action by faith. Activation isn't passive— it requires you to cooperate with God's grace and take intentional steps to stir up what He's placed inside your spirit.

Paul's exhortation to Timothy offers a roadmap for activation: "Therefore I remind you to stir up the gift of God, which is in you by the laying on of my hands" (2 Timothy 1:6).

The phrase "stir up" comes from the Greek word *anazopureo,* which means "to kindle up, to inflame, to reignite." It evokes the image of a fire that hasn't gone out but has diminished in intensity. The embers still glow; they must be fanned into a roaring flame. Paul essentially told Timothy, "Don't let the fire go out. Take action. Fan the flame of your calling."

What does this mean for you? It means you need to engage the gifts God has given you actively. Here are some practical steps to activation:

1. Acknowledge the Gift: Identify what God has placed in your spirit. Spend time in prayer, asking the Holy Spirit to reveal the gifts He has deposited within you. Seek confirmation through trusted spiritual leaders or prophetic voices.

2. Step Out in Faith: Activation requires action. Start using your gift in safe environments where you can build confidence. For example, if God has given you a prophetic gift, begin by sharing simple impressions or words of encouragement with those you trust.

3. Cultivate the Gift: Every gift requires stewardship. This means investing time in study, practice, and prayer. It means seeking God's wisdom on how to refine and grow the gift so it can have the maximum impact.

4. Fan the Flame Daily: Don't wait for someone else to ignite your passion. Take personal responsibility for maintaining spiritual fervor. This may involve praying in the Spirit, meditating on scriptures regarding your gift, or surrounding yourself with others who are on fire for God.

5. Guard Against Fear and Insecurity: One of the enemy's tactics is to keep you paralyzed by fear or doubt, convincing you that you're unworthy or incapable. But remember, the gift is not about your ability—it's about God's power working through you. Step out boldly, trusting Him to work in and through you.

Activation is not a one-time event; it's a lifestyle. The gifts God has placed within you are too valuable to remain dormant. Therefore, continually stir up the gift. Fan the flame if it begins to wane. Step into the fullness of what God has for you, and watch as He breathes on your obedience, igniting a fire that will burn brightly for His glory.

CHAPTER 3

Starter Activations

Stepping into the prophetic doesn't have to feel overwhelming or unattainable. God desires all His people to hear His voice and confidently share His heart with others. However, like any spiritual gift, moving in the prophetic requires intentionality, practice, and, most importantly, faith.

That's why I've included *Starter Activations* in this book—to provide you with a solid, easy-to-follow foundation for taking your first steps in prophetic exercises with confidence and clarity.

The beauty of these starter activations is that they are intentionally designed to be simple and approachable, allowing you to grow at your own pace. Whether you're brand new to the prophetic or looking to rekindle a dormant gift; these exercises will help you build confidence and stretch your faith in hearing and releasing God's voice. They are crafted to break down barriers of fear or doubt that might hold you back.

One of the biggest obstacles many face when stepping into prophetic ministry is the fear of making mistakes. Practicing will help you overcome that fear. These starter activations will also guide you in tuning your spiritual ears, leaning into His presence, and releasing what you sense He is saying. The more you practice, the better you'll recognize His voice with greater clarity.

Think of these exercises as your "training wheels" in the prophetic. You will practice in safe spaces—whether journaling what you sense the Lord is speaking, declaring simple prophetic words over yourself, or stepping out to share an encouraging word with someone. Each activation stretches you just enough to build momentum while keeping you grounded in biblical truth.

As you engage with these starter activations, you'll find your faith growing stronger, your confidence increasing, and your connection with the Holy Spirit deepening. These small, consistent steps will prepare you to step into greater realms of prophetic accuracy and boldness.

Remember this: every prophetic voice that ever existed started somewhere—now it's your turn to take that first step. So, don't hold back. Dive into these starter activations with expectation, knowing that God is eager to meet you where you are. As you begin, trust that He will honor your faith and obedience, equipping you to voice His love and truth.

ACTIVATION 1
Revealing the Great "I AM"

God first revealed Himself as "I AM" in Exodus 3:14: "And God said to Moses, "I AM WHO I AM." And He said, "Thus you shall say to the children of Israel, 'I AM has sent me to you.'"

Jesus later referred to Himself as "I AM" in John 5:8, "Then the Jews said to Him, "You are not yet fifty years old, and have You seen Abraham?" Jesus said to them, "Most assuredly, I say to you, before Abraham was, I AM."

What does this mean, exactly? This name, "I AM," is known as the Tetragarammaton, which appears over 6,000 times in the Bible. The Jews consider this to be the only proper name for God, and it is the most common name for God in Scripture. This name of the Lord appears in the Psalms 700 times alone. *Matthew Henry's Concise Commentary* offers this insight:

"A name that denotes what he is in himself, I AM THAT I AM. This explains his name Jehovah, and signifies, 1. That he is self-existent: he has his being of himself. 2. That he is eternal and unchangeable, and always the same, yesterday, to-day, and forever.

"3. That he is incomprehensible; we cannot by searching find him out: this name checks all bold and curious inquiries concerning God. 4. That he is faithful and true to all his promises, unchangeable in his word as well as in his nature; let Israel know this."

PROPHESY

In this prophetic drill, prophesy to someone who the "I AM" is in their life right now and who the "I AM" wants to be for them in this season. For example, you might prophesy, "I AM your healer" or "I AM your strength." After you prophesy who the "I AM" wants to be for them, launch out into prophecy and encourage them to believe God to be for them who they need Him to be.

ACTIVATION 2
Release a 'Rhema' Scripture

Some prophecies are Scripture—verbatim. That may not sound too exciting, but remember that the Word of God is powerful, alive, and active (see Hebrews 4:12).

The Holy Spirit can put the words He has already said in your mouth to edify, comfort, and exhort people. These "Scripture prophecies" are often right-on-time confirmations when someone is trying to make a difficult decision or battling enemy assault. Think about it: the whole Bible is prophetic—Spirit breathed. God doesn't necessarily have to say something He hasn't already said in His Word to make a profound impact on someone's life.

Remember, prophecy is fallible, but God's Word never fails (see Luke 1:37). The writer of Hebrews expressed the power of the Word: "For the word of God is living and powerful, sharper than any two-edged sword, piercing even to the division of soul and spirit, and of joints and marrow, and is a discerner of the thoughts and intents of the heart" (Hebrews 4:12). A Word-based prophecy can greatly impact the life of a believer seeking revelation or an unbeliever who does not yet know the Lord. The Word accomplishes the work. Make no mistake: this is still prophetic, as you received the right word at the right time. Not every prophetic word has to be profound. The Gospel is simple.

I love it when the Holy Spirit highlights a Scripture I can rely on. Anyone who values the Word will appreciate this type of prophecy.

Jesus said, "Heaven and earth will pass away, but My words will by no means pass away" (Matthew 24:35). And Isaiah 40:8 tells us, "The grass withers, the flower fades, but the word of our God stands forever." And Proverbs 30:5 (ESV), "Every word of God proves true …"

When you prophesy God's Word over someone's life as inspired by the Holy Spirit, you can be sure of this: it will not fall to the ground. Isaiah 55:10-12 makes this plain:

"For as the rain and snow come down from heaven, and do not return there without watering the earth, making it bear and sprout, and providing seed to the sower and bread to the eater, so will My word be which goes out of My mouth; It will not return to Me void (useless, without result), without accomplishing what I desire, and without succeeding in the matter for which I sent it."

PROPHESY

Ask the Holy Spirit to highlight a specific scripture for someone—a verse or passage that speaks directly to their current situation, need, or calling. Take a moment to meditate on the Scripture and listen for how God wants to apply it to their life.

Proclaim the Scripture over them, declaring its truth, promises, and power. Release the life and encouragement found in God's Word, and speak it boldly, knowing that His Word will not return void but will accomplish what He desires in their lives! (see Isaiah 55:11)

ACTIVATION 3
Share God's Thoughts

God's thoughts are higher than our thoughts (see Isaiah 55:8), so our minds must be renewed to reflect His thoughts (see Romans 12:2). When we think like He thinks, our prophetic utterances will ultimately be more accurate because our souls are not filtering His words through our biases.

Paul told us to think about whatever is true, whatever is honorable, just, whatever is pure, whatever is lovely, whatever is commendable, anything excellent, and worthy of praise (see Philippians 4:8).

This verse offers a glimpse into how God thinks. Although God sees sin, He views His sons and daughters through the blood of Christ and sees them as seated in Christ through faith. While He does not excuse sin, Christ became sin so that we might be made the righteousness of God in Him (2 Corinthians 5:21). God continuously holds good thoughts about His sons and daughters.

People don't need us to prophesy their sins and shortcomings. Usually, they are painfully aware of where they fall short of the glory of God. It's more beneficial to prophesy about their potential rather than their problems.

Jeremiah 29:11 tells us, "For I know the thoughts that I think toward you, says the Lord, thoughts of peace and not of evil, to give you a future and a hope."

David, an Old Covenant saint, understood this all too well. David wrote, "How precious also are Your thoughts to me, O God! How great is the sum of them! If I should count them, they would be more in number than the sand; When I awake, I am still with You" (Psalm 139:17-18).

And again in Psalm 40:5, David writes, "Many, O Lord my God, are Your wonderful works which You have done; And Your thoughts toward us cannot be recounted to You in order; If I would declare and speak of them, they are more than can be numbered."

Are you getting the picture? God doesn't excuse our poor behavior, but He will forgive it. He is always thinking good things about us. Sometimes, sharing those good thoughts prophetically can inspire someone to overcome their poor behavior.

PROPHESY

Ask the Holy Spirit to reveal God's thoughts toward someone—His heart, intentions, and desires for their life. Take time to listen and discern His perspective, which is always full of love, hope, and purpose.

As you prophesy, share what you sense God is saying about how He sees them, what He values in them, and the plans He has for them. Speak clearly and encourage them, declaring His truth over their identity and future.

Let your words reflect the depth of God's love and the greatness of His plans for their lives.

ACTIVATION 4
Open Your Mouth and Let God Fill It

Often, prophetic individuals desire to receive the entire counsel of God on a subject before they speak to prophesy. However, it rarely works that way—and that's why many people prophesy only occasionally instead of abundantly.

I don't hear every word before I prophesy it. Often, I sense a bubbling up, or I hear a phrase from which I can launch. Then, when I faithfully release what I have received, more begins to flow.

We know in part, and we prophesy in part, according to 1 Corinthians 13:9. If we want to hear the whole story, we'll probably be waiting a long time.

Again, sometimes that "part" Paul spoke of is merely a single word—at least until you release the one word you heard. Similarly, if you are a seer, "you see through a glass darkly" (see 1 Corinthians 13:2). In other words, you may not see a panoramic view of what God is doing, but you get a glimpse of one detail that is significant to the person you are ministering to. (Get my book, *Seer Activations*, for more seer exercises.)

Psalm 81:10 says, "Open your mouth and I will fill it." So, don't be intimidated if you only have a single word. One word can turn someone's entire life around. Usually, as you pray for someone and release that single word, you tap into prophetic rivers that flow freely. You'll be surprised by what happens next.

—

I can't stress this enough. Don't underestimate the power of a single word, even if that's all you receive. Don't argue with God about whether or not to share it. If the word comes from God, it will make an impact. Once again, a single word from God can change someone's life.

God's Word doesn't return to Him void but accomplishes that which He sends it to do (see Isaiah 55:11). However, if you pray in the Spirit or in your own language over the person and begin to release what you have, you will usually hear more.

In other words, when you sow what you have, you prepare the way for God to bring about a prophetic harvest. Don't let the enemy persuade you that what God has given you to prophesy is insignificant.

PROPHESY

Pray in the Spirit. Ask the Holy Spirit to lead you to someone or a situation that needs a word of encouragement, breakthrough, or direction. Without overthinking, open your mouth and begin to speak in faith, trusting God to fill it with His words. The Lord may give you more as you speak. Even if He doesn't, remember that one word could make all the difference. Allow the Holy Spirit to guide your thoughts and phrases. This is an exercise in surrender and trust, stepping into the flow of His Spirit to express His heart in the moment.

ACTIVATION 5
Declare the New Thing in Someone's Life

Even though Ecclesiastes 1:9 emphatically states that there is nothing new under the sun, there are things that are new to us. God has fresh anointings, revelations, perspectives, and more. He has new relationships in mind, new promotions, new levels of glory, and so on. God is always leading us into a new experience.

Isaiah prophesied extensively about new things. In Isaiah 43:18-19, he declared, "Do not remember the former things, nor consider the things of old. Behold, I will do a new thing; now it shall spring forth. Shall you not know it? I will even make a road in the wilderness and rivers in the desert." This is encouraging because it suggests that God creates a path where there seems to be none.

Isaiah also prophesied about new things in Isaiah 48:6: "You have heard; See all this. And will you not declare it? I have made you hear new things from this time, even hidden things, and you did not know them." When we prophesy the new things, we make what was hidden to an individual known—at least in part—and that causes faith to arise.

Many believers feel trapped in a rut. They can't perceive the new thing. While they desire something fresh, they aren't attuned to the voice of the living God sharing His heart and plans with them. A single prophetic word can reveal God's direction for the upcoming season. One prophetic utterance can declare the new thing God wishes to do in someone's life. This can truly make all the difference.

PROPHESY

Ask the Holy Spirit to reveal the "new thing" God wants to do in someone's life. This could be a new season, opportunity, or direction God is leading them into. Listen for insight about the fresh work of God in their life and how He is making a way where there seems to be no way. Prophesy the new thing with boldness. Speak life over the transition.

ACTIVATION 6
Pray in the Spirit and Prophesy

I've been walking in prophetic ministry for decades, yet I continue to pray this prayer: "Lord, make me more prophetic!" And I pray in tongues. I am convinced that the combination of these natural and heavenly language prayers bears fruit—and fruit that remains.

Praying in the Spirit primes the prophetic pump. Praying in the Spirit makes you more sensitive to the Holy Spirit's voice as you set out to minister.

One way you build your faith to prophesy is by praying in tongues. Catch this: We all have the ability as Spirit-filled believers to prophesy words of edification, exhortation, and comfort (see 1 Corinthians 14:3). That is what we call the simple gift of prophesy available to us as the Holy Spirit wills. So, again, while you need equipping, impartation, and activation in the prophetic, you also need to build your faith to prophesy. The greater your faith, the more prolific you will be in prophetic ministry.

The Passion Translation of Romans 12:6 tells us, "So if God has given you the grace-gift of prophecy, activate your gift by using the proportion of faith you have to prophesy."

Of course, you can and should build faith to prophesy by hearing the Word. Paul put it plainly, "So then faith comes by hearing, and hearing by the word of God" (Romans 10:17). But praying in tongues also builds your faith. Meditating on the Word and praying in the Spirit is a one-two punch that will give you more confidence in the accuracy of your prophetic ministry.

Praying in tongues makes you more prophetic because it is one way we keep ourselves stirred up, alert to the movement of the Spirit, and responsive to His leadership. Commit to praying in tongues one hour a day and watch what happens.

Pick up my book, *Tongues of Fire*, to learn more about the benefits of praying in tongues. Also be sure to take Transform, the 90-day tongues prayer challenge at www.schoolofthespirit.tv/courses/tonguesprayer.

PROPHESY

Begin by praying in the Spirit, allowing the Holy Spirit to stir up your faith and align your heart with His. As you pray, ask the Lord to show you someone who needs a word of encouragement, direction, or breakthrough. Continue praying in the Spirit as you wait for insight, then transition into prophecy by declaring what you sense God is saying. Speak boldly, trusting the flow of the Holy Spirit to guide your words, and release life, hope, and God's promises over the person or situation.

ACTIVATION 7
Prophesy Over Yourself

Always remember this: You are your own best prophet. And get this: When you are praying in tongues, you may be unknowingly prophesying your future. See, the Holy Spirit knows all things, including every step on the way to your destiny. The Holy Spirit is the spirit of prophecy, and He can testify through you what Jesus wants to do in your life as you pray in tongues.

Our tongues hold great power. Proverbs 18:21 tells us, "Death and life are in the power of the tongue, and they who indulge in it shall eat the fruit of it [for death or life]" (AMPC). When you speak in tongues, you are speaking words of life over your situations, circumstances—and even your destiny. You may be prophesying into your future life—the future and the hope God has promised His children (see Jeremiah 29:11).

If you sense the Holy Spirit brooding over you as you release your tongues, take Paul's advice in 1 Corinthians 14:13: "Therefore let him who speaks in a tongue pray that he may interpret."

Here's how it works: Pray for the interpretation, then stay silent and wait on Him to reveal His prophetic words. It's up to Him whether He shows you. Sometimes, if we knew what He was prophesying, we would be tempted to get ahead of Him.

Of course, you can prophesy over yourself in your native language. I have prophesied over myself many times. But you can't choose to prophesy over yourself. The Holy Spirit is the source of prophecy, as He shares the testimony of Jesus (see Revelation 19:10). He has to give you the words.

PROPHESY

Take a moment to invite the Holy Spirit to reveal God's heart for your life, your current season, or your destiny. Ask Him to highlight areas where you need correction, encouragement, or revelation. Begin to speak out loud what you sense God is saying about you—declare His truth, His plans, and His promises. He may lead you to prophesy over your identity, your purpose, and your future, calling forth everything God has placed inside you. He may lead you to speak life, favor, and divine alignment and prepare you to walk more boldly in His will!

ACTIVATION 8
Prophesy Over Someone's Finances

God is our provider. He wants to be the King of our personal economy—and the Bible has plenty to say about money. It may surprise you that the Bible mentions money concepts more than 800 times. Ecclesiastes 10:9 tells us, "Money answers everything." That's quite a statement!

We know we cannot serve two masters, for we will either hate one and love the other or be devoted to the one and despise the other. Jesus said we can't serve both God and money (see Matthew 6:24). He who loves money will not be satisfied with money, nor will he who loves wealth with his income, according to Ecclesiastes 5:10.

Nonetheless, if we serve God with our money, our money can serve us well. Many Christians have a wrong perspective on money. Some lean toward greed and covetousness, while others seem to take an unspoken vow of poverty, thinking it's godly to be poor.

Some Christians are not prospering because their soul is not prospering (see John 1:2). Some are not prospering because they are not tithing and giving offerings. Some are not prospering because they have wrong money motivations. Some are not prospering because of a generational curse.

However, many Christians are prospering wildly and funding great Kingdom exploits that will see them reap eternal rewards by storing up treasures in heaven (see Matthew 6:19-21).

Remember, the blessing of the Lord makes rich, and He adds no sorrow to it (see Proverbs 37:21). When we honor the Lord with our wealth, we will find prosperity (see Proverbs 3:9). When we seek Him first—and His righteousness—everything else we need will be added to us (see Matthew 6:33).

PROPHESY

Ask the Holy Spirit to show you someone who needs breakthrough or encouragement in their finances. Spend a moment listening for God's heart regarding their provision, stewardship, and the blessings He desires to release in their life.

The Holy Spirit may lead you to prophesy God's promises of provision, abundance, and wisdom over their finances. He may lead you to speak to any areas of lack, releasing breakthrough and alignment with heaven's economy.

You may also be led to prophesy a directive word on a season of sowing or a season of reaping. You may see a windfall coming or a curse that needs to be broken, and so on. Prophesy with confidence.

ACTIVATION 9
Release a Strength Strategy

Everyone grows "weary in well doing" at some point. One aspect of personal prophecy is to strengthen. But we can go beyond that and prophesy a strength strategy. Specifically, we can prophesy what someone needs to do to step out of their weariness and into His strength.

Isaiah prophesied a strength strategy: "But those who wait on the Lord shall renew their strength; They shall mount up with wings like eagles, they shall run and not be weary, they shall walk and not faint" (Isaiah 40:31).

While Isaiah's prophetic words offer a general strength strategy that will work for "whosoever will," God can give you a more specific strength strategy for a person on the edge of quitting or walking through a tough trial.

You could prophesy a detailed word by the Spirit, or you prophesy a Scripture the Lord puts on your heart to strengthen someone going through rough times. For example, many Scriptures promise strength. We know God wants to move us from strength to strength. He wants us to seek His strength, be strong and courageous, and so on. Paul said, "I can do all things through Christ who strengthens me" (Philippians 4:13).

PROPHESY

Pray and ask the Holy Spirit to reveal a strength strategy for someone—insight into what they need to do or shift to move from weariness or weakness into God's strength. Seek to hear God's encouragement for their situation, focusing on His promises of renewal and empowerment.

Prophesy with gentleness and uplifting words, offering clear steps or a perspective to help them draw from His strength. If you don't receive a specific strategy, share a scripture that resonates as a rhema word for their situation, declaring God's truth and grace over their life. Speak hope and faith, calling them into the fullness of His power and rest!

ACTIVATION 10
Reveal What the Enemy Doesn't Want Someone to See

While God may hide things for our good and until the right time, the enemy hides things—or tries to hide things—so we can't experience the abundant life Jesus died to give us. Put another way, God's motive for hiding things for us is love. The enemy's motive for hiding things from us is to hold us back from a truth that will set us free or advance His will in our lives.

Moreover, the enemy of our soul doesn't want us to see the hidden things, deep things, and secret things God has for us. He wants us to remain in the dark, without the revelation of what God has done, is doing, or plans to do in our life so God is not glorified in and through us.

The enemy is on a mission to steal, kill, and destroy (see John 10:10). He beats people up and beats people down by unleashing sequential attacks that keep them distracted—or even blinded—from God's promises. The enemy, for example, releases relational confusion and financial setbacks and works other wiles to keep people from seeing what God is trying to show them.

Yes, the enemy uses distraction tactics to get God's beloved ones to focus on the mountains, the fires, the valleys—the problems. When someone focuses too much on what the enemy is doing, they can't see what God is doing. When people can't see what God is doing, they lose heart.

Thanks be to God, He can show the prophet or prophetic person what the enemy is hiding by way of a word of knowledge or prophecy. Once people can see what the enemy is hiding, they can release their faith and prayers to walk into God's blessings.

Prophecy can help cleanse the lens of the one from whom the enemy is stealing revelation. Prophecy helps restore sight to one spiritually blinded by the onslaught of fear, uncertainty, and doubt. Prophecy can help someone see a glimmer of light so they can walk by supernatural faith and not just natural sight.

PROPHESY

Ask the Holy Spirit to show you someone in whose life the enemy is working to keep them from seeing what God wants to reveal. Take time to listen for what God desires to show them—whether it's a hidden blessing, opportunity, or divine strategy they haven't yet seen. Once you receive insight, prophesy it over them with boldness and clarity, declaring what God has planned for them.

Next, engage in spiritual warfare prayer on their behalf, asking God to remove any blinders, combat distractions, and clear out any residue preventing them from walking in full spiritual vision. Declare their eyes be opened to see what God has hidden for them and walk in the fullness of His plans!

ACTIVATION 11
Expose Demonic Seeds

There are four aspects to a mature prophetic ministry found in Jeremiah 1:10. Rooting out is a critical instruction in his prophecy.

God can and does use His prophetic word to root out seeds the enemy has planted in someone's soul. We know the enemy sows seeds—lies—among the truth because Jesus spoke about this in a parable. We read it in Matthew 13:24-28:

"Another parable He put forth to them, saying: "The kingdom of heaven is like a man who sowed good seed in his field; but while men slept, his enemy came and sowed tares among the wheat and went his way. But when the grain had sprouted and produced a crop, then the tares also appeared.

"So the servants of the owner came and said to him, 'Sir, did you not sow good seed in your field? How then does it have tares?' He said to them, 'An enemy has done this.'"

Catch that: "An enemy has done this." Satan is the father of lies (see John 8:44). He planted seeds in the soul of Eve in the Garden. He planted seeds in the mind of Judas, who betrayed Jesus. He plants seeds in our minds.

Indeed, the enemy plants seeds in the souls of believers and unbelievers alike. If you can see the lie, you can combat it with the truth through a clear prophetic word from the mind of Christ.

PROPHESY

First, practice on yourself. Ask God to show you the enemy's seeds of doubt, fear, or lies that may have taken root in your mind. As He reveals these seeds, begin by prophesying to yourself, rooting out these lies, and replacing them with the truth of God's Word. Declare over your own life the truth that sets you free, pulling down strongholds and demolishing false beliefs.

Once you have broken free, look for opportunities to help others by discerning the lies they are believing. You don't need to point out the lie directly; instead, prophesy the truth that will set them free, speaking life and light into the darkness and declaring the truth that roots out every lie the enemy has sown!

ACTIVATION 12
Prophesy the Latter that's Greater

You've heard it said—and sung—"your latter being greater than your past." Those are encouraging words, but when you understand the ultimate context of these words, it will give you faith to wait for the latter.

The original context is in the Book of Job, the first book written in terms of Bible history. (Genesis appears first, but Job wrote his book before Moses penned the Pentateuch.)

Job 8:7 reads, "Though your beginning was small, yet your latter end would increase abundantly." These weren't Job's words. They came from the mouth of Job's "friend" Bildad the Shuhite. Bildad was calling Job to repentance. Although Job's friends were hardly friends— they were judgmental rather than merciful—Job eventually did repent in Job 42. (But not for that which his friends accused him.)

Long story short, God restored Job and gave him double for his trouble. Job's latter truly was greater than his past. *The New Living Translation* of Job 8:7 reads, "And although you started with little, you will end with much." One translation reads, "From your modest beginnings, the future will be bright before you."

Sometimes, people need to repent—not of sin but of failing to trust God during a destructive trial, trauma, or tragedy. "Repent" at its root means to change the way you think.

According to *The KJV New Testament Greek Lexicon*, the word for repent, "metanoeoe," means: "to change one's mind, i.e., to repent; to change one's mind for the better, heartily to amend with abhorrence of one's past sins."

A prophetic word can help people see their need to trust God for Romans 8:28 and Genesis 50:20. Often, it's our repentance—changing the way we think—that opens the door to double our trouble.

PROPHESY

Ask the Holy Spirit to reveal what God wants to do in someone's latter years, even if they have had a fruitful or successful past. Prophesy how their latter will be greater than their past. In other words, press in to hear the Holy Spirit and get as specific as you can about what God will do in their later years.

God may lead you to prophesy hope and encouragement, reminding them that He has greater things ahead, even amid challenges. Prophetic words about our latter days can stir up faith and motivation, giving people a fresh vision for what's to come and urging them to press on with purpose, knowing that God's best is still ahead.

ACTIVATION 13
Bless Your Way Into Prophesying

In a Nigerian church in London, I experienced something I had never witnessed before. After laying hands on at least one thousand people to release the seer anointing, the entire congregation turned and started blessing me in unison.

These thankful believers stretched their hands toward me and continued for five minutes, saying: "I bless you. I bless you. I bless you. I bless you." I could feel the blessings of God. It was quite something.

Releasing a blessing is powerful. God told Abram, "I will bless those who bless you, And I will curse him who curses you; And in you all the families of the earth shall be blessed" (Genesis 12:3). The Hebrew word for bless in that verse is, well, bless.

Bless means to speak well of, to approve, to confer prosperity and happiness upon someone. It also means to favor. God is a God of blessing, and He wants His prophetic word to bless people. Blessing someone is one gateway into the prophetic flow. Since blessing is the heart of God for His people, this gateway helps you tap into His mind about how He wants to bless them.

In Deuteronomy 28:3-6, we see some of the blessings of obedience God promised the Israelites: "Blessed shall you be in the city, and blessed shall you be in the country. Blessed shall be the fruit of your body, the produce of your ground and the increase of your herds, the increase of your cattle and the offspring of your flocks. Blessed shall be your basket and your kneading bowl. Blessed shall you be when you come in, and blessed shall you be when you go out."

PROPHESY

Begin by praying God's blessings over someone—bless their body, bless their mind, bless their finances, and bless their relationships. Use these blessings as a gateway to invite the Holy Spirit to reveal more specific insights.

As you bless them, listen carefully for what the Lord wants to bless more specifically or what He would say about the next blessings He has in store for their life. Expect that blessing flow to naturally transition into a prophetic word. God may lead you to prophesy His favor, breakthrough, and specific promises over their life. This will not only release blessings but also open the door for deeper prophetic insight as you bless their future.

ACTIVATION 14
Declare the Blessing in the Trial

When we walk through trials, we often feel anything but blessed. We feel attacked. We feel angry. We feel scared. But we usually don't feel blessed. However, James, the apostle of practical faith, insists that we are blessed.

James 1:12 (NIV) tells us plainly, "Blessed is the one who perseveres under trial because, having stood the test, that person will receive the crown of life that the Lord has promised to those who love him."

The New Living Translation says, "God blesses those who patiently endure testing and temptation. Afterward, they will receive the crown of life that God has promised to those who love him."

Often, when we're in a trial, we don't know why. We may blame ourselves, but it's not always our fault that we end up in unfavorable or unbearable circumstances. Sometimes, it's what people do or do not do us that births a trial.

What's more, the enemy can bring adversity into our lives, and God, at times, will give us tests just like He did with Abraham. No matter the source of the discomfort, we're often walking so closely to it or are so overwhelmed by it that we can't see our way through it. We don't see the blessing in the trial.

But what if you could see the outcome? What if you could see the promotion? What if you could see the restoration? What if you could see what God saw? When people walk through serious trials, they don't need Job's friends to call them to repent. They don't need pat answers, either.

When people go through trials, they need to hold on to the anchor of hope. The prophetic word can bring hope for a better tomorrow—hope for an outcome that makes the trial bearable.

PROPHESY

Find someone going through a trial—whether it's in their marriage, at work, in their finances, or with their health. As you listen to their struggle, begin to pray for them and seek God's perspective on what He is doing in them and for them through this trial.

Ask the Holy Spirit to reveal how it will work out for their good. Prophesy with encouragement, declaring what God is accomplishing in their life through this difficult season. Prophesy the outcome of this trial— perhaps it's the strength they will gain, the wisdom they will acquire, and the breakthrough that will come as they walk through it with faith.

ACTIVATION 15
Release the Generational Blessing

For all the talk of generational curses—which are very real—we should be mindful to prophesy the generational blessing. In fact, once a generational curse is broken, generational blessings often begin to manifest in someone's life because the barrier is removed.

What is a generational blessing? It's a blessing that passes from one generation to the next. We see generational blessings throughout Scripture. These are blessings that may have started in your family line hundreds of years ago and pass to you and through you to your children.

Psalm 145:4 tells us: "One generation shall praise Your works to another, and shall declare Your mighty acts." Psalm 100:5 promises: "For the Lord is good; His mercy is everlasting, and His truth endures to all generations." Psalm 119:90 reveals: "Your faithfulness endures to all generations; You established the earth, and it abides."

Psalm 112:2 tells us: "His descendants will be mighty on earth; The generation of the upright will be blessed." And Psalm 71:18 insists: "Now also when I am old and grayheaded, O God, do not forsake me, until I declare Your strength to this generation, your power to everyone who is to come."

PROPHESY

Ask God to reveal the generational blessings that are in your family line. These could be blessings of favor, inheritance, health, prosperity, wisdom, or spiritual gifts that have been passed down through the generations. Begin by prophesying these blessings over yourself, declaring that you are aligned with God's covenant promises. Speak into your life and your family's life, declaring the manifestation of these blessings.

Next, ask the Holy Spirit to show you someone else who needs to receive a generational blessing. Prophesy these blessings over them. Call forth the fullness of what God has established for their family line, and release the blessings that will flow from generation to generation!

ACTIVATION 16
Prophesy Over Someone's Business

Some people have an apostolic anointing in the marketplace. They are Kingdom builders rather than ministry builders. Or, put another way, their ministry is to build the Kingdom through witty inventions and generous offerings as their God-inspired ventures prosper. This is a vital aspect of the Kingdom.

In the Parable of the Talents, after Jesus called ten of His servants and gave them money to put to work, He said, "Engage in business until I come" (Luke 19:13, ESV). Other versions say, "conduct business" or "do business." He wasn't just talking about a Christian bookstore. A secular business can hold a Kingdom purpose.

God wants to prosper Kingdom-minded business owners, and give them strategies to release the power to create wealth and wisdom in business dealings (see Deuteronomy 8:18). God wants to give them witty inventions and novel ideas (Proverbs 8:12). By contrast, the enemy wants to steal, kill and destroy Christian businesses (see John 10:10). So there's a war going on.

Sometimes, business owners need a prophetic word to wage war with (see 1 Timothy 1:18). Sometimes, they need a word that confirms the major leap of faith they are preparing to take. Sometimes, they need a strategy they can't see because of the stress of spiritual warfare.

PROPHESY

Ask the Holy Spirit to show a business owner to prophesy over. This could be someone you know or someone God highlights to you in daily life. Press in and listen for specific words of encouragement, strategies, or promises for the person's business. What does God want to accomplish through this business? What area of breakthrough does God want to bring? Is there a word of wisdom or strategy God is releasing? Prophesy!

ACTIVATION 17
Expose the Devil's Strategy to Devour

Peter tells us the enemy is roaming about like a roaring lion seeking someone he may devour (see 1 Peter 5:8). He's looking for someone with an open door of attack who will tolerate his lies and fall for his deception. And sometimes he doesn't need an open door. He attacks to open a door! (Jesus had no open door and the enemy attacked Him!)

God prophesied through Malachi that if we tithe and give offerings, God will rebuke the devourer. Have you ever wondered what that means? Simply put, rebuke means rebuke!

When we think of a rebuke, we think of a reprimand or a sharp criticism. But rebuke in this context is that and more. *Merriam-Webster* defines rebuke as "to turn back or keep down." One of the definitions for the Hebrew word rebuke is "corrupt." God will corrupt the enemy's plans.

The New Living Translation of Malachi 3:11 puts it in plain English: "Your crops will be abundant, for I will guard them from insects and disease. Your grapes will not fall from the vine before they are ripe," says the Lord of Heaven's Armies."

It's helpful to know, though, what the enemy is seeking to devour. The good news is that God can show you the enemy's devouring agenda so that someone can stand against it, pray against it, and otherwise come into agreement with God's plan for blessing and abundant life.

PROPHESY

Ask the Holy Spirit to reveal an area in someone's life where the enemy seeks to steal, kill, or destroy. This could be related to their health, relationships, finances, ministry, or destiny. Press in to discern what the enemy is targeting, and then listen for God's heart and His promises for restoration, protection, and breakthrough. Release His Word to shut down the enemy's plans and align the person's life with His purposes!

ACTIVATION 18
Prophesy Someone's Reward

Scripture tells us God is a rewarder of those who diligently seek Him (see Hebrews 11:6). And that's not the only reason why God hands out rewards.

Colossians 3:23-24 reminds, "And whatever you do, do it heartily, as to the Lord and not to men, knowing that from the Lord you will receive the reward of the inheritance; for you serve the Lord Christ." And Ephesians 6:5-8 drives it home:

"Bondservants, be obedient to those who are your masters according to the flesh, with fear and trembling, in sincerity of heart, as to Christ; not with eyeservice, as men-pleasers, but as bondservants of Christ, doing the will of God from the heart, with goodwill doing service, as to the Lord, and not to men, knowing that whatever good anyone does, he will receive the same from the Lord, whether he is a slave or free."

God is a rewarder. He rewards both good and evil. I could go on and on about this. He releases rewards to us in His timing and the right season. If we don't grow weary in doing well, we will reap a harvest of rewards (see Galatians 6:9). Of course, only what we do with the right motives counts. When love motivates us, we can be assured of a reward.

PROPHESY

Ask the Holy Spirit to reveal a reward God has prepared for someone faithful in their walk, ministry, or assignment. Listen for insight about the seeds they have sown, the battles they have fought, or the sacrifices they have made. Press in to hear how God is bringing increase, breakthrough, or restoration in their life. Then prophesy the reward, speaking encouragement and hope, and declare the manifestation of God's promises over their obedience and faithfulness!

ACTIVATION 19
Declare God's Mercy

Mercy is one of the attributes of God's character. It's part of who He is. He never stops being merciful. Even in judgment, He remembers mercy (see Habakkuk 3:2). True prophets carry a mercy gift as they speak the heart of the Father. Jesus said, "Be merciful, even as your Father is merciful" (Luke 6:36).

God invites us to experience His mercy. Hebrews 4:16 tells us plainly: "Let us therefore come boldly to the throne of grace, that we may obtain mercy and find grace to help in time of need."

We need mercy daily, which is why God's mercies are new every morning (see Lamentations 3:22-23). God has plenty of mercy to go around. He is rich in mercy because of His great love for us (see Ephesians 2:4-5). He wants us to be merciful, too, and promises us a blessing when we are. Jesus said, "Blessed are the merciful, for they shall obtain mercy" (Matthew 5:7).

We all need mercy, which essentially means a blessing that is an act of divine favor or compassion or compassionate treatment to those who are in distress. Many people beat themselves and receive the enemy's condemnation when they aren't perfect. Prophesy the mercy of God into someone's life.

PROPHESY

Ask the Holy Spirit to show you someone who needs a fresh revelation of God's mercy. This could be someone burdened by guilt, shame, condemnation, or a difficult season. Press in to hear God's heart for them and how His mercy is reaching into their situation. Prophesy as specifically as possible areas of their life where He wants them to receive His mercy.

ACTIVATION 20
Prophesy a New Name

"Your new name is Grace." Those were the words of a prophet friend of mine. He came to minister at Awakening House of Prayer, my South Florida church. Behind the scenes, he gave that word to one of my staff members. She was touched deeply.

God gave people new names in Scripture several times. Simon was turned into Peter, and Jacob was turned into Israel. Saul was turned into Paul. Abram was turned into Abraham. Sarai was turned into Sarai. Name changes have to do with identity.

At the leading of the Lord, you may prophesy a new name over someone. Keep in mind, that doesn't necessarily mandate someone is going to go to an attorney and get a name change. (That was a trend in the 1990s!) Rather, it's just a name the Holy Spirit wants them to adopt as part of their identity in Him.

Peter was the rock. Jacob shed his schemer profile. Abraham was the father of many nations. Grace, as it turns out, was going to be a name my friend needed to remember because of the trials she endured and many more trials she was about to go through.

Interestingly, Revelation 2:17 says, "To him who overcomes I will give some of the hidden manna to eat. And I will give him a white stone, and on the stone a new name written which no one knows except him who receives it."

—

PROPHESY

Ask the Holy Spirit to reveal the new name God is speaking over someone—a name that reflects their identity, calling, or destiny in Him. Listen for a name that represents how God sees them, not how they see themselves or how others have labeled them. Prophesy this new name with boldness. God may lead you to declare the significance and transformation the new name brings. Speak life over their identity, calling them into alignment with who God says they are and the plans He has for their future!

ACTIVATION 21
Prophesy to the Dry Bones

In Ezekiel 37, God commanded the prophet to prophesy to the dry bones. It must have sounded like a strange directive, but when God picks you up and sets you down in a valley full of dry bones, I imagine one is compelled to obey.

Once the prophet was in the valley, the next thing God did was locate his faith to prophesy. That's important because we prophesy according to the proportion of our faith (see Romans 12:6). To locate Ezekiel's faith, God asked: "Son of man, can these bones live?" (Ezekiel 37:3). Ezekiel didn't quite have the faith to prophesy just yet. I imagine the site was overwhelming to the physical senses. Ezekiel rightly answered, "O Lord God, You know" (Ezekiel 37:3).

That's when God told Ezekiel, "Prophesy to these bones, and say to them, 'O dry bones, hear the word of the Lord! Thus says the Lord God to these bones: "Surely I will cause breath to enter into you, and you shall live. I will put sinews on you and bring flesh upon you, cover you with skin and put breath in you; and you shall live. Then you shall know that I am the Lord'" (Ezekiel 37:4-6).

I like that. Prophesy as you are commanded by faith. Then, after you prophesy and see the results, you'll have more faith. When we prophesy and see the manifestation of what we released, it builds our faith for the next assignment.

Look for the dry bones God wants you to prophesy over. Prophesy by faith, not by sight.

PROPHESY

Ask the Holy Spirit to reveal areas in someone's life where they are experiencing spiritual dryness or lifelessness. These could be areas of their health, relationships, dreams, finances, or emotional state.

As you discern these areas, take a moment to reflect on Ezekiel 37, where God speaks life into the dry bones. Let this passage stir your faith as you prepare to prophesy.

Begin by declaring God's will for restoration and healing over these dry areas. Prophesy to the "dry bones" in their life, commanding them to live again by the power of God's Spirit. Call forth God's creative power to breathe life into every dead area, just as He did with the dry bones.

Prophesy the restoration and transformation God wants to bring into their life. Speak God's truth over them, knowing that His Word has the power to bring life where there was none.

ACTIVATION 22
Prophesy the Battle's Outcome

After massive warfare against the rebuilding of the Temple in Jerusalem, King Darius showed the Israelites favor. After years of opposition, he found King Cyrus' former decree that allowed the Jews to build the temple debt-free—at the expense of the foreign kingdom. This was an encouragement, but there was still work to be done.

Ezra 6:14-15 reads, "So the elders of the Jews built, and they prospered through the prophesying of Haggai the prophet and Zechariah the son of Iddo. And they built and finished it, according to the commandment of the God of Israel, and according to the command of Cyrus, Darius, and Artaxerxes king of Persia. Now the temple was finished on the third day of the month of Adar, which was in the sixth year of the reign of King Darius."

Catch that: They prospered through the prophesying of prophets. This is in line with 2 Chronicles 20:20, "Believe in the Lord your God, and you shall be established; believe His prophets, and you shall prosper."

Ever wonder what they were prophesying? Everything seemed to be going well, so why did the prophets need to prophesy at that point?

MacLaren's Expositions says, "these two prophets did more for building the Temple by their words than an army of labourers with their hands." The prophets

53

encouraged them to continue the work through the many years of warfare, and now continued to inspire them on the last leg of the journey.

When the Lord shows you someone is in a battle, prophesy the potential, prophesy the outcome, and prophesy encouragement that keeps them from quitting.

PROPHESY

Ask the Holy Spirit to bring to your heart someone currently walking through a long battle, whether in their health, finances, relationships, or spiritual life. Spend a moment in prayer, asking God for His perspective on the situation. As you receive insight, begin to prophesy to that person words of encouragement.

God may lead you to speak life over their weary heart, or remind them that God is with them and will sustain them through the battle. God may inspire you to prophesy that the victory is on the horizon, even if they cannot see it yet. God may lead you to encourage them that this battle is not in vain and that He is refining and preparing them for something greater.

ACTIVATION 23
Re-prophesy a Word

We've spent much time in prophetic ministry foretelling, but forthtelling is also part of prophetic ministry. Forthtell means "to make public" or to "publish abroad," according to *Merriam-Webster*'s dictionary. You could also say to "tell forth." One aspect of forthtelling is to say what God has already said. I call it re-prophesying the word.

There is so much emphasis on predicting in the prophetic realm, and that's valid, but what about prophesying the word God already gave until people respond to it? Also, consider this: the Lord will sometimes lead prophets and prophetic people to release the same word that another prophet issued a decade ago because the danger is impending or the opportunity is present.

John Paul Jackson's *Perfect Storm* message is a great example. People are re-issuing his warnings, as well as David Wilkerson's. You can re-prophesy the warning, as led by the Spirit. You can keep decreeing it until it lands on ears that hear. People re-prophesy Smith Wigglesworth's word about a revival of the Word and the Spirit.

This is biblical. Peter re-prophesied the prophet Joel's words in Acts 2:17-18: "'And it shall come to pass in the last days, says God, that I will pour out of My Spirit on all flesh; your sons and your daughters shall prophesy, your young men shall see visions, your old men shall dream dreams. And on My menservants and on My maidservants I will pour out My Spirit in those days; and they shall prophesy.'"

Be careful, though, to be led by the Spirit to re-prophesy something. Don't pick up a word and claim it as yours. And don't re-prophesy a word out of God's timing. Just because God said it once doesn't mean He's saying it to the next group who gathers. Just because it sounds deep doesn't mean it's the right word in another setting.

Be a student of prophecy like Daniel (see Daniel 9:2). Pray the prophecy through. If God wants you to, you can re-prophesy it.

PROPHESY

Ask the Holy Spirit to lead you to a prophetic word that was prophesied in the past—even the ancient past—that is a "now" word in this season. This may be a word from Scripture or the past generation.

Take time to reflect on this prophetic word and ask God to show you how it needs to be re-prophesied in this season. You might be re-prophesying the warning to encourage action or shift someone's course, or you might be speaking a word of encouragement to remind someone that what God spoke still stands. Always credit the original source.

As you re-prophesy, speak it with fresh faith, understanding that God's words do not return void. Declare His promises again, and speak His warnings in love, urging alignment with His will. Trust that, as you speak, the word will have the same power and impact it had when it was first given, and that it will stir faith, change, or conviction in those who hear it. This is not just about reiterating past words but forthtelling—making what God has already said alive again in the present moment.

ACTIVATION 24
Prophesy Against Doubt in the Heart

Our heart is our innermost being, that's why God tells us to guard our heart with all vigilance, for out of it flow the issues of life (Proverbs 4:23). We know the pure in heart shall see God (Matthew 5:8). Man looks at the outward appearance, but God sees the heart (see 1 Samuel 16:7).

Many people feel misunderstood. Many are heartbroken. Many have desires in their hearts that have not yet come to pass, and they wonder if they missed God. Others have plans in their hearts that have been delayed, and they need confirmation that they haven't missed God—or what is hindering the manifestation of the promise.

The Lord weighs the heart (Proverbs 21:2). He searches the heart and tests the mind (see Jeremiah 17:10). He doesn't want our hearts to be troubled (see John 14:27). He wants us to love Him and seek Him with our whole hearts (see Psalm 119:10). He wants to impart wisdom to our hearts (see Psalm 90:12). He wants us to have a heart of courage (see Psalm 31:24). He never wants our hearts to fear (see Psalm 27:3).

Only God knows what is in someone's heart— expectation, discouragement, hope, etc. —but He can show you what is in their heart so you can strengthen, confirm, or redirect them to His heart. A prophetic word can bring healing to a broken heart and revelation to a confused soul.

PROPHESY

Take a moment to quiet your spirit and open your heart to receive from God. Ask the Holy Spirit to reveal any areas of doubt that have crept into someone's heart—places where fear, delay, or discouragement have tried to take root. Are there promises they have struggled to believe? Are there areas where they have questioned if they truly heard from God? The Holy Spirit may lead you to release words of courage, faith, and confirmation. He may direct you to break off the enemy's lies and speak assurance over delayed promises. Let the Spirit lead as you release words of life and boldness.

ACTIVATION 25
Write Out & Analyze a Prophetic Word

Many times in Scripture, we see, "for thus it was written by the prophet…" The Old Testament prophets wrote—or chronicled—prophetic words so that generations after could learn lessons, expect God's purpose to manifest, or receive divine warnings.

For example, Daniel found a prophecy from Jeremiah about the end of Israelite captivity and that led him to seek the Lord for what was next. Joel prophesied the outpouring on Pentecost, and Peter said, "This is that." And, of course, many Messianic prophecies point to the First and Second Comings of Christ.

You don't have to release prophecies of end times proportions to put this principle into place. You'd be surprised how quickly you forget what God said to you if you aren't intentional to scribe it. Write down the prophetic words God speaks to you and analyze them. Look up the meanings of the words God speaks to your heart—or for others—in the dictionary. Look them up in Scripture.

In this way, you are deeply analyzing what God said so that you can prepare yourself—or the people over whom you are prophesying—to walk out the prophecy. Since most prophecies are conditional, there is a process between the promise and the fulfillment. Some processes are faster than others. Put another way, the prophetic word always needs a response. Sometimes, that's preparation. Other times, that's a massive action to step into the word in the fullness of time.

PROPHESY

Take a moment to reflect on a recent prophetic word you received or released. Write it down in detail. As you do, ask the Holy Spirit to help you understand the meaning behind each part of the word.

Once you have it written out, go back and analyze it. Is there a theme or a specific message that stands out? What scriptures or principles come to mind? Ask God for clarity on anything that might seem unclear.

Prophesy over that word again, declaring it shall come to pass in God's perfect timing and with His full provision. Revisit your prophetic words regularly and allow the Holy Spirit to continue to unpack deeper layers of understanding. This will build confidence in hearing God's voice more clearly and stewarding prophetic revelation.

ACTIVATION 26
Release Words of Preservation

God is a God who defends and preserves. The very word preservation means "to keep safe from injury, harm, or destruction." Preserve means "to protect, to keep alive, intact, or free from decay."

Moses was a prophet of preservation. Hosea 12:13 tells us, "By a prophet the Lord brought Israel out of Egypt, and by a prophet he was preserved." David understood that God is a God of preservation. In Psalm 138:7 (ESV), he wrote, "Though I walk in the midst of trouble, you preserve my life; you stretch out your hand against the wrath of my enemies, and your right hand delivers."

By contrast, the enemy comes to steal, kill, and destroy (see John 10:10). We need to be Christ-focused, but we also need to be on the lookout for a lurking enemy seeking to devour so we can stand guard. The enemy comes to destroy marriages, kill businesses, and steal dreams. God wants to preserve His will in the lives of His people.

The psalmist cried out, "Guard me, O Lord, from the hands of the wicked; preserve me from violent men, who have planned to trip up my feet" (Psalm 140:4, ESV).

PROPHESY

Ask the Holy Spirit to show you someone who needs God's preservation power to manifest in their life—whether it's their health, finances, family, or even their purpose and calling.

—

Take a moment to reflect on the areas where God's protection, preservation, and provision are needed. Listen closely to God's heart and His promise of keeping and guarding His people.

As you sense God's direction, begin to prophesy His words of preservation over them. He may lead you to prophesy how He is preserving them in a specific area of their life, whether it's guarding their heart, providing for their needs, or keeping them safe from harm. He may lead you to speak words of protection over their health, family, and destiny, declaring that no weapon formed against them will prosper.

ACTIVATION 27
Ask God to Tell You a Secret

Anybody who has been around prophets and prophetic ministry is more than a little familiar with Amos 3:7-8: "Surely the Lord God does nothing unless He reveals His secret to His servants the prophets."

Those are strong words! God doesn't do anything unless at least one person on the earth knows what He's up to. Before God sent fire and brimstone down on Sodom and Gomorrah, He asked, "Shall I hide from Abraham what I am doing, since Abraham shall surely become a great and mighty nation, and all the nations of the earth shall be blessed in him?" (Genesis 18:17)

God did tell Abraham, and Abraham went into intercession. Nobody else but Abraham knew what God was about to do because it was a secret. A secret is something kept from common knowledge or view. It's hidden, undercover, designed to elude observation or detection, a mystery, and shared confidentially.

Everyone—yes, even God—has secrets. Choosing whether to—and to whom—a secret is revealed rests solely in the power of the secret holder. Knowing secrets can make us feel special, especially when they are God's secrets. But with a secret comes a responsibility. Many times, that responsibility is intercession.

PROPHESY

Quiet your heart and invite the Holy Spirit to reveal something hidden—ask God to tell you a secret. This could be about a person, a situation, or a deeper understanding of His plans. Open your heart and mind to hear, trusting that God delights in sharing His secrets with those who seek Him (see Amos 3:7).

Ask the Lord to reveal His heart and to guide you into a deeper level of intimacy with Him. Be still and allow space for Him to speak, whether through a thought, a picture, a scripture, or an impression. Listen for any details, revelations, or divine insights He wants to share with you.

Once you have received something from the Lord, thank Him for His faithfulness and cherish the secret He has entrusted to you. If He leads you, prophesy what you've received, whether it's encouragement for someone else or direction for a situation. But remember, you can only share His secrets with those to whom He leads you. Some secrets are for intercession only.

—

ACTIVATION 28
Who Can But Prophesy?

"A lion has roared! Who will not fear? The Lord God has spoken! Who can but prophesy?" (Amos 3:8) This is an intriguing question—and an intriguing Scripture. Have you ever given it much thought? What does this mean?

We know the spirit of the prophets is subject to the prophets (see 1 Corinthians 14:32), which means we can choose to prophesy or not. Even if there is "fire in our bones," as Jeremiah described, we can choose not to open our mouths and release that prophetic fire. God will not violate our free will.

But, like Jeremiah, Amos had a hard time resisting the urge to prophesy. This wasn't a slight unction or a faint impression. This was like a bold lion within him waiting for the opportunity to release the roar—the prophecy.

Pulpit Commentary says, "As the lion's roar forces everyone to fear, so the Divine call of the prophet forces him to speak."

There's a time when, even if you don't want to, the Holy Spirit will compel you to prophesy with such force that it would be an absolute sin not to share His words in your mouth.

Often, when we have this feeling, it's because it's a difficult word. It's a word that's not popular. It's a word that will make some angry and position the prophet for persecution. Or, it's a word of warning that's so imminent that the Lord will not let you sleep until you release it. One warning: Be careful not to mistake your roar for His.

PROPHESY

Take a moment to meditate on the powerful question from Amos 3:8: "Who can but prophesy?" Ask the Holy Spirit to ignite a prophetic fire within you as you stand in agreement with the call to prophesy.

Begin by inviting the Holy Spirit to open your ears to hear God's voice and your heart to respond with boldness. Ask God to show you someone or something that needs to hear His word today. It may be a word of encouragement, wisdom, or direction. As you feel the Holy Spirit prompt you, allow the prophetic flow to rise within you.

Prophesy with boldness. As you prophesy, remember that the Spirit within you compels you to speak what God reveals. Stand in the boldness of His calling, knowing that when God speaks, His voice is powerful, and you are a vessel through which His prophetic word flows.

Embrace the question, "Who can but prophesy?" with the understanding that as His people, we are all called to speak what He shows us even when it's uncomfortable. Step out in faith, knowing that the Spirit will guide and empower you to prophesy with accuracy and authority.

ACTIVATION 29
Prophesy to the Heart

The Bible speaks repeatedly about the heart. God wants to encourage our hearts, purify our hearts, share wisdom with our hearts, and more.

We are to love God with all of our heart (see Matthew 22:27). God looks at our heart (see 1 Samuel 16:7). The Lord searches the heart (see Jeremiah 17:10). The heart reflects the person (see Proverbs 27:19).

God calls us to store up His Word in our hearts (see Psalm 119:11). We are told to delight ourselves in Him and He will give us the desires of our heart (see Psalm 37:4). We are to seek Him with our whole heart (see Psalm 119:10). Where our heart is, our treasure will be also (Matthew 6:21).

With so many Scriptures speaking about the heart, God may just offer you a Scripture to share with them. God is the strength of their heart (see Psalm 73:26). We are to trust in the Lord with all our hearts (see Proverbs 3:5).

PROPHESY

Ask the Holy Spirit to reveal someone whose heart needs encouragement, healing, or a touch from God. Take a moment to reflect on the significance of the heart in Scripture—how God desires to encourage, purify, and speak wisdom to our hearts (Proverbs 4:23, Matthew 5:8). As you pray, ask God to show you His heart for the person and any specific areas where their heart may need His intervention.

As you receive insight, begin to prophesy to their heart. God may lead you to speak words of comfort, healing, and encouragement. He may lead you to declare that their heart will be made strong, that it will know the peace of God, and that God will give them wisdom and understanding for their life. He may lead you to prophesy that His love will heal any discouragement or pain in their heart and that His light will shine brightly within them.

Trust that as you prophesy to their heart, God's healing and wisdom will take root, and they will be strengthened in their inner being to walk in His peace and purpose.

ACTIVATION 30
Declare God's Wonderful Works

Our God is a wonder-working God. Psalm 111:1-4 tells us, "The works of the Lord are great, studied by all who have pleasure in them. His work is honorable and glorious, and His righteousness endures forever. He has made His wonderful works to be remembered."

Our God is a Wonderful Counselor (see Isaiah 9:6). God multiplied His signs and wonders in Egypt (see Exodus 7:3). The Lord did wonders among the Israelites in the wilderness, bringing them into the Promised Land (see Joshua 3:5)

Job 9:10 tells us, "He does great things past finding out, Yes, wonders without number." 1 Chronicles 16:24 says, "Declare His glory among the nations, His wonders among all peoples."

And David said, "Many, O Lord my God, are Your wonderful works Which You have done; And Your thoughts toward us Cannot be recounted to You in order; If I would declare and speak of them, They are more than can be numbered" (Psalm 40:5). And again, "You are the God who does wonders; You have declared Your strength among the peoples" (Psalm 77:14). David also said, "Wonderful are your works; my soul knows it very well" (Psalms 139:14).

God's wonderful works can deliver you—He saved Daniel from the lion's den and saved Shadrach, Meshach and Abednego from being burned alive. God's wonderful works can prosper you——Jesus paid Peter's taxes by leading him to catch a fish with coins in its mouth. God's wonderful works calm the storms in our lives. God's wonderful works reconcile marriages that seemed beyond repair. God's wonderful works supernaturally cancel debt—and more.

PROPHESY

Begin by reading and meditating on Psalm 111:1-4, which speaks of God's wondrous works and the awe they inspire. Reflect on His greatness and the marvelous things He has done throughout history, in your own life, and the lives of others. Ask the Holy Spirit to open your eyes to see the wonders of God in your current circumstances or in the lives of those around you.

As you focus on God's mighty works, ask the Holy Spirit to reveal specific wonders He has done or is about to do. Then, begin to prophesy about His works.

God may lead you to prophesy about the miracle He wants to perform in someone's life. That may include works of healing, deliverance, provision, or relational reconciliation. He may lead you to prophesy words of encouragement or to remind someone of His ability to intervene and perform the miraculous in their lives.

ACTIVATION 31
Prophesy God's Favor

Many years ago, I was on the phone with Cindy Jacobs, discussing my transition from serving as the first-ever female editor of *Charisma* magazine to full-time ministry. Out of nowhere, she made a prophetic announcement, "You are in a season of crazy favor." Suddenly, it was like a switch flipped, and there was favor, favor everywhere. I walked and am still walking in the favor of God and man.

David said in Psalm 5:12, "For You, O Lord will bless the righteous; With favor You will surround him as with a shield." And again, "Let the favor of the Lord our God be upon us, and establish the work of our hands upon us; yes, establish the work of our hands!" (Psalm 90:17, ESV). And Psalm 30:5 says God's favor is for a lifetime. Imagine that.

Favor is something God gives us. We can't earn it or buy it. Favor is undeserved. It's a gift. Favor is God's gracious kindness. Paul spoke of God's kind intentions toward us, and David spoke of God's precious lovingkindness. It's part of God's nature to favor His people. He is love and love is kind. The Holy Spirit is the spirit of grace.

Favor is a special privilege or right granted or conceded. Because you have favor, you can go boldly to the throne of grace to obtain mercy and find grace to help in times of need. Favor means to show partiality toward. Favor means to give support or confirmation to. God is a very present help in times of need (see Psalm 46:1).

Favor means to afford advantages for success. Everything you put your hand to prospers. Favor means in one's good graces. That means God thinks highly of you. He sees you through the blood of Christ. You don't have to be perfect to walk in crazy favor.

Favor means permission and leniency. Favor is preferential treatment. God is predisposed to bless you. Do you know how airlines let active duty military get on the plane first? That's preferential treatment. That's favor.

PROPHESY

Begin by taking a moment to focus your heart on God's goodness and His ability to release favor. Ask the Holy Spirit to guide you as you seek God's heart for someone in need of favor—whether it's for their finances, relationships, career, or ministry. Listen for any insight God wants to give you about how He desires to show favor to them in this season.

Once you hear His voice, prophesy God's favor over them in specific areas. Aim to prophesy the specific favor He wants to shower on them in this or an upcoming season. That may look like supernatural opportunities, unexpected blessings, or divine connections.

ACTIVATION 32
Build Your Faith to Prophesy

Some people have more faith to prophesy than others. Some of that faith comes from experience in the prophetic. It is sort of like riding a bike; when you first start out prophesying, you may be a little nervous. You may even fall. But once you have become more experienced, you can ride with no hands or pop a wheelie. You're confident.

Remember, another word for faith is "confidence." We need to be confident in our prophetic utterances. But what if you are just starting? How do you build your faith? Or what if you've been prophesying for over a decade, but God brings you to another level, and demon powers are dogging you with insecurities?

That's where Romans 12:6 comes in. Paul tells us in this verse: "Having then gifts differing according to the grace that is given to us, let us use them: if prophecy, let us prophesy in proportion to our faith."

What does that mean?

Some translations say, "Speak with as much faith as God has given you" (NLT). The Amplified Bible says, "in proportion to the faith possessed." Other translations say, "amount of faith" or "measure of faith" or "according to the faith you have."

One way to build your faith to prophesy is to meditate on the Word of God. Romans 10:17 tells us, "So then faith comes by hearing, and hearing by the word of God." Faith comes by hearing the Word of God over and over again. The more you hear the Word of God, the more your mind is renewed to His voice and His will and His ways—and the more confident you'll be in prophesying. What Scriptures are you meditating on?

PROPHESY

Take a moment to reflect on your current level of faith to prophesy. Building faith to prophesy starts with acknowledging that the prophetic is a gift from God and that He desires to speak through you.

Start by reading scriptures that build your faith in God's ability to speak to you. Reflect on how God has spoken to others in the Bible and how He is still speaking today. Allow these scriptures and testimonies to ignite a greater faith that you, too, can hear His voice and release His words.

Practice by prophesying over small things in your life—your relationships, your ministry, or even your personal journey. Speak words of life, encouragement, and direction over yourself, building your confidence to hear and prophesy with accuracy.

Trust that as you build your faith, your ability to prophesy will grow. Step out in boldness, knowing that the Holy Spirit is always with you, empowering you to speak God's truth into any situation. The more you prophesy, the more your faith will increase, and the clearer God's voice will become to you.

ACTIVATION 33
Check Your Heart

While most prophetic drills look outward, this exercise aims inward. Here it is: Before you prophesy to others, check your heart.

It's possible to rise in prophetic ranking despite your hidden character flaws, but you won't be able to maintain your position if you don't minister God's way. (Check out my course on Prophetic Ranks & Authority at *www.schoolofthespirit.tv*). The Bible says if the Lord isn't building the house we are laboring in vain (see Psalm 127:1). Well, the Lord isn't going to build a prophetic lighthouse to the nations on a foundation with character cracks. He has to deal with the cracks first so the lighthouse doesn't fall over later.

If you want to prophesy over nations, if you want to impact the lives of the masses, if you hope to be a general in the great company of prophets and intercessors the Lord is raising up, then you need to fill up the cracks in your character with the fruit of the Spirit. You need to purify your prophetic flow now because the Bible says what we do in secret will be shouted from the rooftops. In other words, your unrepented, habitual, justified sin will find you out. It's just a matter of time.

The devil is strategic. He waits until you can influence tens of thousands of people and then plays the trump card—that character flaw that you never dealt with—and pulls the rug out from under your ministry and all those who trusted in it.

Over the years we've seen scandals disgrace prophets and leave hurting people to pick up the pieces. I continue to watch believers who fall prey to merchandising prophets who leave them with empty pockets and empty promises. I've seen behind the curtain and it's anything but God's will for the prophetic. This is a vital ministry and we must take the responsibility to purify ourselves so the devil can find nothing in us. Examine yourself.

PROPHESY

Take a moment to pause and ask the Holy Spirit to examine your heart. Ask God to reveal any areas that need purification or alignment. The state of your heart is crucial in prophetic ministry, as it must be free from offense, bitterness, or impurity to hear clearly from God and represent Him rightly.

Specifically, ask the Holy Spirit to show you any areas where your heart might be hardened, distracted, or misaligned with His will. Listen carefully, and if anything comes to mind—unforgiveness, fear, or hidden motives—bring it before the Lord in repentance.

Ask the Holy Spirit to purify your heart and remove any hindrances to hearing His voice. Ask Him to soften your heart and remove anything that could distort or hinder your ability to prophesy with accuracy, love, and purity. Once you have aligned your heart, ask the Holy Spirit to fill you with His Spirit once again.

ACTIVATION 34
Be a Student of the Prophets

Are you a student of the Word? If you want to cultivate an accurate spirit, you should be. In the Old Testament, the "school of the prophets" wasn't a place to study how to prophesy. No, the schools of the prophets founded by Samuel and Elijah were a place to study the Word of God.

Every prophet or prophetic person needs to be a student of the whole counsel of God, as well as the Old Testament and New Testament prophets. Some Old Testament prophets wrote entire books, while the prophecies of Elijah and Elisha, among others, are tucked in other books of the Bible. The ministries of other prophets, like John the Baptist and Ananias, are found in the New Testament Gospels and epistles.

Being a student of the prophets helps you understand God's ways related to prophetic ministry. You'll see the differences and similarities between the Old Testament and New Testament prophets. You must understand those differences so you don't prophesy out of an Old Testament-only paradigm.

Ultimately, being a student of the prophets is being a student of the Word. Jesus called the Word of God our bread (see Matthew 4:4). Job said it was his necessary food (see Job 23:12). When we feast on the Word, we are building our faith to prophesy and renewing our minds so we will better discern His will.

David called the Word of God a lamp unto His feet and a light unto His path (see Psalm 119:105). The Word leads you down the right path and away from spirits of error and divination. Paul said the Word of God is the source of our faith (see Romans 10:17). We prophesy according to the proportion of our faith, so we need to study the Word to show ourselves approved (see 2 Timothy 2:15).

PROPHESY

If you hope to consistently and accurately prophesy with authority, you must be grounded in the Word of God. The more you immerse yourself in Scripture, the clearer God's voice will become, and the more confident you will be in releasing His prophetic words. Take time today to be a student of the prophets—a student of the Word. Commit to spending time daily in the Bible—let it become your anchor.

Ask the Holy Spirit to open your eyes to deeper revelation as you read about the prophets. Let the Word transform you, sharpening your ability to discern the voice of God from other voices in the spirit realm—and even your soul. As you study, meditate on verses that speak to you, and journal the insights you receive. Ask God to show you how His Word applies to the prophetic words He's giving you.

ACTIVATION 35
Discern False Prophecy

Prophecy is either right or wrong—or partially right and partially wrong. But false prophecy is more than sincerely wrong. It can be misleading and manipulating—and that's dangerous.

Yes, you—or someone else—can release a word that has some truth in it and some error in it. Sometimes people put a comma where God put a period. In other words, they continue prophesying after God has stopped talking. That makes it part God and part soul. But that's still not a "false prophecy."

We need to be well-versed in discerning both wrong and false prophecy, whether it comes from our mouths or someone else's mouth. But start with yourself. If you can't discern error in your prophecy, you may not discern error in someone else's prophecy. That means you are deceived and potentially deceiving others—and you may not even know it. That's a scary thought!

To discern wrong or false prophecy, you need to be a student of the Word of God and the ways of God. You need to know His nature and His emotions. You need to renew Your mind. Just because the prophecy sounds good—and to take it a step further, even though the prophecy sounds like God—doesn't mean it came from God.

Wrong prophecy can come from a fervent heart. It can come from carnal desires. It can come out of biases, rejection, hurts, and wounds. Certainly, you would never set out to prophesy wrongly. But that doesn't mean it's not possible. And some people do set out to prophesy falsely. Remember, false doesn't just mean wrong. It means intentionally untrue. False prophecy aims to mislead.

Take Paul's advice, "But test all things carefully [so you can recognize what is good]. Hold firmly to that which is good" (1 Thessalonians 5:21, AMPC). You'll be glad you did. If you discern you have heard wrongly, there's still time not to prophesy wrongly. Thoroughly test your prophecy before releasing it—and always test the prophecy you hear.

REFLECT

Take a moment to ask the Holy Spirit for discernment as you reflect on any prophetic words you've received or heard recently. The Bible warns us that there will be false prophets, and we must be vigilant in discerning the truth from the counterfeit.

Begin by asking God to sharpen your spiritual senses. What within the content of the prophetic word you heard didn't sit right in your spirit? Ask the Holy Spirit to reveal any areas where the word did not align with Scripture or did not bring peace to your heart. Trust that God will guide you in distinguishing between the genuine and the false.

Spend time meditating on the fruits of the Spirit and the nature of God's true voice. False prophecy often manipulates, causes confusion, or leads away from truth.

True prophecy brings clarity, peace, and alignment with God's will.

Pray for a greater sensitivity to the Holy Spirit's promptings. Ask Him to help you test every word against Scripture and His character. Use discernment to reject any word that does not align with the truth of God's Word and what He's already spoken over your life.

For more on judging prophecy, pick up my book, *Did the Spirit of God Say That?* Or check out my prophetic training courses at SchooloftheSpirit.tv.

ACTIVATION 36
Discern False Prophets

Like the demons that inspire them, false prophets have been roaming about seeking to fleece unsuspecting sheep since Moses walked the earth—or at least God has been warning us about these pseudo-ministers since then.

Yes, modern-day false prophets are operating in counterfeit anointings. When Jesus walked the earth, He warned, "Beware of false prophets, who come to you in sheep's clothing, but inwardly they are ravenous wolves" (Matthew 7:15).

No, they don't come dressed as sheep, but they do prey like wolves. And if they do pray, they often pray witchcraft prayers. (Witchcraft prayers align with their will rather than God's will.) Sadly, too many believers are falling for the false hope of false prophets and sowing into their coffers, thereby enabling them to continue their false ministries and deceive more desperate sheep.

Discernment is needed in the Body of Christ as many are enamored with accurate words of knowledge and predictive prophecies. We must test the spirits speaking. John the Beloved wrote, "Dear friends, do not believe everyone who claims to speak by the Spirit. You must test them to see if the spirit they have comes from God. For there are many false prophets in the world" (1 John 4:1, NLT).

So what can we take away from this? 1. There are many false prophets. 2. It's up to us to discern the truth from falsehood. 3. We have to judge prophecy.

The devil always counterfeits what's real. The New Testament mentions false prophets eleven times. Jesus talked about them, Peter talked about them, and John talked about them. The Old Testament mentions false prophets over and over again. Just as there are characteristics of true prophets, there are clear signs of false prophets.

PROPHESY

Whether in person or over social media, false prophets are becoming more prevalent, and it's essential that we, as prophetic people, are equipped with the discernment to recognize them. Begin by asking the Holy Spirit to heighten your sensitivity to His voice. Ask Him to help you to distinguish the true from the false in every situation.

As you reflect, consider the characteristics of a false prophet. Do they lead people away from Scripture? Are they driven by self-promotion or manipulation? Do their words create division or confusion? True prophets speak in alignment with God's Word and bear fruit that edifies, exhorts and comforts.

—

When you encounter a prophetic word or a self-proclaimed prophet, ask the Holy Spirit to help you sense the spirit behind the message. Is there peace in your spirit, or does something feel off? God's voice brings peace and clarity, not confusion or manipulation. Test what you hear and see, especially on social media, against the truth of Scripture. False prophets often twist the Word for personal gain, but true prophets bring God's message with humility and integrity.

Pray for wisdom and boldness to speak truth and protect yourself and others from false influence. Trust that the Holy Spirit will guide you to discern accurately and guard your heart against the subtle deception of false prophets.

For more on this topic, pick up my trilogy, *Discerning Prophetic Witchcraft, Exposing Prophetic Witchcraft,* and *Deliverance from Prophetic Witchcraft.*

ACTIVATION 37
Exhort Someone Prophetically

Paul the apostle wrote, "But he who prophesies speaks edification and exhortation and comfort to men" (1 Corinthians 14:3).

The Greek word for "exhortation" in this verse is "paraklesis." According to *The KJV New Testament Greek Lexicon*, it means: a calling near, summons; importation, supplication and entreaty; exhortation admonition and encouragement; consolation, comfort, solace, that which affords comfort or refreshment; persuasive discourse, stirring address, instructive, admonitory, conciliatory, powerful hortatory discourse.

Merriam-Webster's dictionary defines exhortation as "the act or instance of exhorting; language intended to incite and encourage." Exhort means "to incite by argument or advice: urge strongly; to give warnings or advice, to make urgent appeals."

We see God, the source of all true prophecy, exhorting Joshua to "be strong and of good courage, for you will bring the children of Israel into the land which I swore to them, and I will be with you" (Deuteronomy 31:23).

In Acts 11:22-24, we see Barnabas, a New Testament prophet, operating in exhortation and the fruit of that exhortation:

"News of these things came to the ears of the church which was in Jerusalem, and they sent Barnabas to Antioch. When he arrived and saw the grace of God, he rejoiced and exhorted them all to remain with the Lord with a loyal heart. For he was a good man, full of the Holy Spirit and of faith. And many people were added to the Lord."

PROPHESY

Start by asking the Holy Spirit to highlight someone who needs some exhortation. It could be someone you know personally or someone God brings to your attention in prayer. Ask God to show you how He wants to exhort that person. What do they need to hear right now? What truth will strengthen their faith and help them press forward?

Once you receive prophetic insight, speak it out. God may lead you to prophesy who they are in Christ or to remind how God sees them and the value they carry. He may lead you to prophesy His promises. He may lead you to prophesy about their potential, not just their present circumstances. He may lead you to prophesy the victories they've already experienced and the greater things ahead. Of course, He may also lead you to give them a warning.

Your prophetic exhortation can build their faith and stir them to action, motivating them to take the next step toward God's calling.

ACTIVATION 38
Prophesy to Build Up

Yes, prophecy can root out, throw down, tear down and destroy but it can also build up—or edify. Paul the apostle wrote, "But he who prophesies speaks edification and exhortation and comfort to men" (1 Corinthians 14:3).

The Greek word for "edification" in this Scripture is "oikodomoe." According to *The KJV New Testament Greek Lexicon*, it means (the act of) building up, building up; edifying, edification, the act of one who promotes another's growth in Christian wisdom, piety, happiness and holiness.

Merriam-Webster's dictionary defines edification as "an act or process of edifying." And edify means to build, establish, and instruct and improve especially in moral and religious knowledge. It also means to uplift, enlighten and inform.

Let's look at some Scriptural references for how prophecy builds up:

"Then Zerubbabel the son of Shealtiel and Joshua the son of Jozadak rose up and began to build the house of God which is at Jerusalem, and the prophets of God were with them, helping them" (Ezra 5:2).

Building is hard work. The prophets were there to encourage the builders in the journey, prophesying God's heart. We see how well this worked in Ezra 6:14:

"The rebuilding by the elders of the Jews prospered through the prophesying of Haggai the prophet and Zechariah the son of Iddo."

In the church at Antioch, we also see prophets moving in edification: "Judas and Silas, being prophets themselves, exhorted the brothers with many words and strengthened them" (Acts 15:32). Paul wrote, "Therefore I write these things being absent, lest being present I should be sharp, according to the authority which the Lord has given me for edification and not for destruction" (2 Corinthians 13:10).

Ephesians 4:29 tells us, "Let no unwholesome word proceed out of your mouth, but only that which is good for building up, that it may give grace to the listeners."

If that's true for every believer, how much more for someone speaking in God's name? Would God defy His suggestion? The simple gift of prophecy should release grace to the listeners.

PROPHESY

Take a moment to ask the Holy Spirit to bring someone to mind who needs to be built up. It could be someone facing discouragement, doubt, or walking through a trying season. Ask God to share with you what they need to hear. You may not receive all the answers, but the Holy Spirit will give you a few words to start. When you release what He gives you, typically more will flow.

He may lead you to prophesy words that will stir their faith and ignite their hope. Maybe that's declaring that they are more than conquerors, that they are equipped for every challenge they face, or that God is working in them and through them. Follow His lead.

When you prophesy to build up, you are laying a foundation for them to stand strong, to press forward, and to walk in the fullness of God's call for their life. Be bold and speak with authority, knowing that the Spirit-inspired words you release have the power to transform their thinking, to restore their hope, and to propel them toward their destiny.

ACTIVATION 39
Share a Word of Comfort

The Holy Spirit is our comforter, so it only makes sense that part of the gift of prophecy is to comfort. Paul the apostle wrote, "But he who prophesies speaks edification and exhortation and comfort to men" (1 Corinthians 14:3).

The Greek word for "comfort" in this verse is "paramuthia." According to *The KJV New Testament Greek Lexicon*, the word means "any address, whether made for the purpose of persuading, or of arousing and stimulating or of calming and consoling; consolation, comfort."

Merriam-Webster's dictionary defines comfort as "to give strength and hope to; to ease the grief of trouble of." Given that the Holy Spirit is the spirit of prophecy and our Comforter, this is one of the easiest aspects of the simple gift of prophecy to understand.

The Holy Spirit is our comforter according to John 14:16 and John 14:26, and since He's the one who is giving us the gift of prophecy, wouldn't it make sense His words would be comforting? Consider the nature of God in relation to comfort, even when we don't deserve it:

"As one whom his mother comforts, so I will comfort you" (Isaiah 66:13).

"I, even I, am He who comforts you" (Isaiah 51:12).

"Even though I walk through the valley of the shadow of death, I will fear no evil; for You are with me; Your rod and Your staff, they comfort me" (Psalm 23:4).

"For whatever was previously written was written for our instruction, so that through perseverance and encouragement of the Scriptures we might have hope" (Romans 15:4).

"When I said, 'My foot slips,' Your mercy, O Lord, held me up. When there is a multitude of worries within me, Your comforts delight my soul" (Psalm 94:18-19).

"The Spirit of the Lord God is upon me because the Lord has anointed me to preach good news to the poor; He has sent me to heal the broken-hearted, to proclaim liberty to the captives, and the opening of the prison to those who are bound; to proclaim the acceptable year of the Lord and the day of vengeance of our God; to comfort all who mourn…" (Isaiah 61:1-2).

The Bible tells us to comfort one another: "So comfort yourselves together, and edify one another, just as you are doing" (1 Thessalonians 5:11).

And when it comes to prophecy, Paul wrote, "For ye may all prophesy one by one, that all may learn, and all may be comforted (1 Corinthians 14:31).

PROPHESY

Take a moment to ask the Holy Spirit to highlight someone who needs God's comfort. It could be someone grieving, walking through a fiery trial, or facing a giant. Ask God to reveal words from His heart that will bring them peace and reassurance.

As you listen, prophesy God's comforting words over them. He may lead you to speak His peace into their situation. That may sound like prophesying that He is with them, that He has not forgotten them, and that His love will see them through. You might prophesy how He will bring them through this season. He knows what they need to hear. Yield to Him.

ACTIVATION 40
Prophesy What God Wants to Restore

It's been said that God is a God of restoration. That's true, but it means so much more than you think. Consider this: When you restore something, you return it to its original condition or position. Restoration can be a simple repair. I got a nail in my tire the other day. The tire shop restored it with a patch.

But God's restoration is greater than man's restoration. When God restores, He doesn't just return something to its original condition. He makes it better. With my tire example, that could mean a new tire. And not just a new tire, but like the best tire in the shop. And not just one tire because it's not good to change one tire on a car. But two—or even four—tires!

Many Scriptures speak of God as a God of restoration. Isaiah 61:7 says, "Instead of your shame you shall have double honor, and instead of confusion they shall rejoice in their portion. Therefore in their land they shall possess double; Everlasting joy shall be theirs."

Consider Joel 2:25-26, "So I will restore to you the years that the swarming locust has eaten, the crawling locust, the consuming locust, and the chewing locust, My great army which I sent among you. You shall eat in plenty and be satisfied, and praise the name of the Lord your God, who has dealt wondrously with you; and My people shall never be put to shame."

And again, look at Zechariah 9:11-12, "As for you also, Because of the blood of your covenant, I will set your prisoners free from the waterless pit. Return to the stronghold, You prisoners of hope. Even today I declare that I will restore double to you."

PROPHESY

Take a moment to ask the Holy Spirit to show you what God wants to restore in someone's life. It could be their health, relationships, joy, or anything the enemy stole. Allow God to reveal areas that need divine restoration.

Once you sense His leading, begin to prophesy restoration in that area. He may lead you to speak a promise of renewal over the broken relationships. He may lead you to prophesy about an area He's healing in their heart or redemption for what has been stolen or destroyed.

Prophesy with faith, knowing that God's can restore anything. Nothing is beyond His ability to restore, and that He is faithful to bring beauty from ashes.

—

ACTIVATION 41
Prophesy What God Wants to Turn Around

God is a God of turnaround. He can take ashes and make something beautiful (see Isaiah 61:3). He takes what the enemy meant for harm and turns it for our good (see Genesis 50:20).

A turnaround is a change for the better. A divine turnaround is when God interrupts the course of natural events abruptly or surprisingly. Think of the Israelites leaving Egypt. The Red Sea was in front of them, and the Egyptian army was behind them. God split the Red Sea and built walls of water to create a tunnel of sorts so the Israelites could walk across on dry land. When all the Israelites had crossed over, the water closed in and drowned the enemy (see Exodus 14).

A barren woman named Hannah saw a divine turnaround after Eli, the priest, accused her of being drunk while she was crying out to God in prayer at the altar. Eli recognized his error and came into agreement with her prayers. The barrenness was broken and she ultimately birthed six children (see 1 Samuel 1:6-7-2:1).

Think of Peter and his partners after they had fished all night and caught nothing. Their livelihood was dependent on a haul of fish. Jesus came on the scene and instructed Peter to "throw the net on the other side." The result: They brought in such a haul of fish that their once-empty boats were suddenly overflowing, and the nets were breaking (see Luke 5:1-10).

Proverbs 13:12 says, "Unrelenting disappointment leaves you heartsick, but a sudden good break can turn a life around."

PROPHESY

Ask the Holy Spirit to reveal a situation that God wants to turnaround for someone. It could be a personal struggle, a challenging relationship, a financial burden, or any situation in which they feel stuck or hopeless. Wait on the Lord to show you where He wants to release His turnaround power.

Once you receive prophetic insight, begin to prophesy by faith. God may lead you to prophesy what He is turning around for good. He may lead you to prophesy life and hope into the area in someone's life that feels dead. You may prophesy about situations where God is breaking through with His power and bringing breakthrough. Prophesy with confidence, knowing that God specializes in turning hopeless situations into testimonies of His greatness.

ACTIVATION 42
Reveal What God Wants to Pour Out

God is a God who pours. God can pour out many things—and wants to in His timing. Peter re-prophesied the words of the Old Testament prophet Joel in Acts 2:17:

"And it shall come to pass in the last days, says God, that I will pour out of My Spirit on all flesh; Your sons and your daughters shall prophesy, your young men shall see visions, your old men shall dream dreams."

Paul noted how God poured out the Holy Spirit on us abundantly through Jesus Christ (see Titus 3:6). God also poured out His Spirit on the house of Israel (see Malachi 3:10). But it's not just His Spirit He pours out. God's pour speaks to His generosity. In Malachi 3:10, God said:

"'Bring the whole tithe into the storehouse, that there may be food in my house. Test me in this,' says the Lord Almighty, "and see if I will not throw open the floodgates of heaven and pour out so much blessing that there will not be room enough to store it."

God can pour out any blessing we need. He pours out blessings on the obedient. He pours out mercy to the repentant sinner. He pours out grace to those who believe. God can pour out wisdom liberally (see James 1:5). He pours out understanding. He pours out His love, shedding it abroad in our hearts by the Holy Ghost (see Romans 5:5).

God pours out gifts and callings, which are irrevocable (see Romans 11:29). But God can also pour out correction, disciplining those He loves (see Hebrews 12:6). And one day, on the wicked who refuse to repent, He will pour out His wrath on the wicked.

PROPHESY

Ask the Holy Spirit to reveal what God wants to pour out on a specific person, place, group, or church. It could be His presence, provision, a fresh anointing, or a new season of breakthrough. Wait on the Lord until you receive the revelation of what God desires to release.

Listen closely for the specifics of what He wants to pour out. Is it an outpouring of His Spirit, a greater level of favor, healing, wisdom, or revival? Ask God to show you how He wants to bless and equip the person for the next season.

Once you have clarity, begin to prophesy with boldness. Release the prophetic announcement by faith, knowing that God is faithful to pour out exactly what is needed in this season.

ACTIVATION 43
Prophesy a 'Now' Word

Some prophetic words predict the future—they foretell what is to come. But some words are what I would call "now" words.

A "now" word deals with the present time or moment—or a time immediately to follow. A "now" word deals with current events in someone's life. A "now" word shows what is already in progress.

God can be doing something right under our noses—something that eye has not seen, nor ear heard, nor entered the heart of man (see 1 Corinthians 2:9)—and we don't immediately perceive it. Other times someone can be in a crisis or a lengthy trial and find it difficult to hear what the Holy Spirit is saying to them. Still, other times, God surprises them with an unexpected blessing.

Scripture says, "Now faith is..." (see Hebrews 11:1). Prophesying a "now" word can bring "now faith" for someone to take God's next step or encourage their hearts that God is an on-time God. Joel prophesied a "now" word to Israel in Joel 2:12, "Now, therefore," says the Lord, "Turn to Me with all your heart, with fasting, with weeping, and with mourning."

Isaiah also prophesied a "now" word: "Come now, and let us reason together," says the Lord, "Though your sins are like scarlet, they shall be as white as snow; Though they are red like crimson, they shall be as wool" (see Isaiah 1:18).

PROPHESY

Quiet your heart and invite the Holy Spirit to speak to you about someone who needs a "now" word—a word that speaks to what He wants to do for them in this very moment. God is always working, and He desires to reveal His current plan and purpose. Don't look ahead or behind—focus on what He is doing at this moment.

What is God's immediate plan? What does He want to release, shift, or reveal at this very time? Be still and listen, trusting that God will give you specifics.

Once you receive the word, prophesy. Speak into their current season. Prophesy what God is doing now or is about to do—even if it doesn't make sense to your mind. For example, He may lead you to prophesy about a "now" breakthrough. He may lead you to prophesy healing is being released now. Speak with authority, knowing that God's timing is perfect.

ACTIVATION 44
Release a Romans 8:28 Prophecy

One of my all-time favorite Scriptures is Romans 8:28, "And we know that all things work together for good to those who love God, to those who are the called according to His purpose."

Look at the *Amplified Bible*, which puts it even stronger: "And we know [with great confidence] that God [who is deeply concerned about us] causes all things to work together [as a plan] for good for those who love God, to those who are called according to His plan and purpose." And *The Passion Translation* puts it this way: "So we are convinced that every detail of our lives is continually woven together for good, for we are his lovers who have been called to fulfill his designed purpose."

Many people have a hard time believing this when calamity, trials, and tribulation suddenly strike their lives—or when they have made grave mistakes that took them out of God's will and brought negative consequences in their lives. Condemnation loves to seep into the souls of believers who missed God.

That's when a prophetic voice can come in with encouragement that God is still working. God makes a way out of no way. God is not a man that He should lie. Ecclesiastes 3:11 tells us, "He has made everything beautiful in its time." And Jeremiah 29:11 (NLT) promises, "For I know the plans I have for you," says the Lord. "They are plans for good and not for disaster, to give you a future and a hope."

PROPHESY

Take a moment to ask the Holy Spirit to highlight an area in someone's life that God is about to turn for good. It could be a strained relationship, a season of emotional distress, or a past disappointment that needs God's Romans 8:28 promise. Ask God to show you what He is working out behind the scenes and how He intends to use it for His glory and their good.

As you focus on the person or situation, begin to listen carefully for what God wants to do. It may be that God is turning pain into purpose, a setback into a setup for greater breakthrough, or a season of struggle into a season of strength. Once you sense what God wants to turn for good, begin to prophesy.

CHAPTER 4

Intermediate Activations

Once you've built confidence with starter activations, it's time to stretch your faith and take your prophetic gifting to the next level. Intermediate activations are designed to challenge you in new ways, sharpening your discernment and expanding your ability to hear and deliver the Word of the Lord. These exercises will move you beyond the basics, helping you recognize and release God's heart with greater precision and depth.

At this stage, you're no longer simply testing the waters; you're stepping deeper into the prophetic flow. These intermediate activations will require you to take risks, lean more heavily on the Holy Spirit, and trust what you're sensing, even when it feels unfamiliar. God is faithful to meet you in these moments of vulnerability, and every time you step out in obedience, your spiritual senses become sharper, your confidence increases, and your faith grows stronger.

The intermediate level is about refining your prophetic voice and learning to navigate the nuances of prophetic ministry. You may start encountering areas where you need to improve accuracy, timing, or delivery. That's part of the process. Don't be discouraged if you feel stretched—growth often happens outside of our comfort zones. These activations are not about perfection but about learning to trust God more deeply and releasing His Word with humility and faith.

It's also essential at this level to practice in community. Sharing what you sense with trusted mentors or fellow believers will help you grow in accountability and receive valuable feedback. God often confirms His Word through others, and practicing together can be a powerful way to sharpen your gift.

Remember, the goal of these intermediate activations isn't just to grow in skill but to cultivate a deeper relationship with the Holy Spirit. Every step you take in obedience draws you closer to His heart, enabling you to speak His words with greater boldness, compassion, and authority.

So, lean into these intermediate activations with anticipation. God is ready to take you higher, deeper, and further than you've gone before. This is your opportunity to stretch, grow, and step boldly into the prophetic calling on your life.

ACTIVATION 45
Prophesying the Condition to the Prophetic Manifestation

Like many of the 7,000 promises we find in the pages of Scripture, many prophecies—in fact, most personal prophecies—are conditional. For example, Jesus says, "Give, and it will be given to you" (Luke 6:38). The "giving to you" is dependent on you doing something first. The "giving to you" is conditional upon your giving.

Likewise, Proverbs 2:1-5 tells us, "My son, if you receive my words, and treasure my commands within you, so that you incline your ear to wisdom, and apply your heart to understanding; Yes, if you cry out for discernment, and lift up your voice for understanding, if you seek her as silver, and search for her as for hidden treasures; Then you will understand the fear of the Lord, and find the knowledge of God."

Can you see the condition of this promise? It's multifaceted: (1) receive my words; (2) treasure my commands within you; (3) incline your ear to wisdom; (4) apply your heart to understanding; (5) cry out for discernment; (6) lift up your voice for understanding; (7) seek wisdom as you would silver; (8) search for wisdom as if looking for a hidden treasure." That's a lot of conditions!

Many prophetic voices prophesy a promise as a "done deal" when the receiver must often do their part to bring God's will into manifestation. Although the condition may be implied, if the condition is not explicitly expressed, some recipients may mistakenly believe the prophetic word will come to pass with little or no effort on their part. They believe the prophecy will come true no matter what they or anyone else does or does not do. That's just not true. So when the prophecy fails to manifest, oftentimes, the prophet is accused of releasing a false prophecy.

Let me give you an example: If I prophesy God will send you to China as a missionary, there are implied conditions. You need to get a passport and learn something about the culture. You need to begin to prepare yourself spiritually and to pray for China before you get there. You may need to work to establish contacts in China. You need to build your faith. Get it?

Of course, conditions on prophetic promises should be common sense in many cases, especially with directive words. I am not saying every prophecy needs to include specific steps. I am pointing out that some believe a prophetic word comes to pass nearly automatically over time if it is truly the word of the Lord. They take a "wait and see" approach. This is not the standard in New Testament prophecy.

There are almost always conditions to personal prophecy. Start training yourself to prophesy with God's conditions in mind. Listen for His conditions rather than blanketly prophesying every prophetic promise as if it's a done deal.

Remember, faith without works is dead (see James 2:26). People can believe the prophets, but if they don't act on that belief, they may not prosper through the promise.

PROPHESY

Pray for someone and ask God to give you a prophetic word for them. But don't stop there. Ask God if there are any conditions on the prophetic promise. If so, be sure to prophesy the conditions.

You might prophesy, for example, "If you rise early in the morning to pray, I will reward you with more revelation and authority." This way, the person to whom you are prophesying understands how to activate God's prophetic promise in their life and can put their faith in the outcome.

ACTIVATION 46
Reveal Elohim's Creative Purposes

God is *the* Creator. In the beginning, He created the heavens and the earth (see Genesis 1:1). He created man in His own image. He created the plants and land animals. He created the sun, the moon and the stars. He created the birds and sea creatures. He created it all.

Indeed, Hebrews 11:3 tells us the universe was created by the word of God so that what is seen was not made out of things that are visible. God literally spoke everything into existence. Think about that!

Speaking of Jesus, Colossians 1:16 (NLT) tells us, "For through him God created everything in the heavenly realms and on earth. He made the things we can see and the things we can't see—such as thrones, kingdoms, rulers, and authorities in the unseen world. Everything was created through him and for him."

Elohim, our creator God, is finished creating the world but that doesn't mean He is out of the creation business. He's still doing "new things"—things He purposed for our lives before the foundation of the earth (see Isaiah 43:19). And He's still creating through us.

Ephesians 2:10 tells us we were created in Christ Jesus for good works, which God prepared beforehand for us to walk in. 1 Timothy 4:4 assures us everything created by God is good.

Prophetic words carry creative power because they are birthed from the very breath of God. The same God who spoke the universe into existence works through His prophets to decree His will on the earth. Prophetic words don't just inform—they transform. They shift atmospheres, birth new realities, and align people with God's purposes.

When we speak the words of God, we are speaking spirit and truth—life. We are calling those things that are not as though they were, according to Romans 4:17. We are speaking the will of God into lives, families, businesses, cities, or nations.

PROPHESY

Ask the Holy Spirit to reveal the creative purposes Elohim, the Creator God, has designed for someone's life. Listen for insight into the gifts, talents, and unique callings He has placed within them. Press in to hear how God wants to use their creativity to bring glory to Him, whether through art, innovation, problem-solving, or building His kingdom.

Prophesy the release of their creative potential. Prophesy what God is creating for a person, corporation or ministry. Prophesy God's creative purposes for the next season so they can come into agreement with Elohim.

ACTIVATION 47
Expose the Enemy Stronghold

God can and does use prophecy to help people identify strongholds in people's minds. Strongholds are lies that have blinded people to the truth and hold them in some measure of bondage.

Although the simple gift of prophecy is edification, exhortation, and comfort (see 1 Corinthians 14:3), sometimes lies must be torn down before people can be built up with the word of the Lord. In other words, sometimes, the enemy's lies prevent them from receiving, embracing, and walking in God's truth. If a stronghold is causing people to struggle in life, the truth will set them free, comfort them, and help them rebuild their lives on Christ.

Remember, a prime prophetic function is to root out and to pull down, to destroy and to throw down, according to Jeremiah 1:10. If we keep prophesying to someone's potential but never prophesy to expose and dismantle the enemy's stronghold in their mind, they may never see God's purpose, believe who they are in Christ and walk in their high calling.

Prophetically identifying enemy strongholds is a more advanced expression of the prophetic—and your words must be seasoned with grace. Remember, the Word of God divides between soul and spirit and exposes our innermost thoughts and desires (see Hebrews 4:12). If the yoke-breaking prophecy is truly coming from God's heart, then it will expose what opposes the truth just as does the written Word of God.

Many people have no idea how the enemy is influencing their minds. If they can't discern the enemy's imaginations combating their soul, they won't cast them down in compliance with 2 Corinthians 10:5. The stronghold will hold them back.

Once the enemy's lies are exposed, freedom and breakthroughs can manifest. Once the strongman is revealed, people can take back what the devil stole. The truth sets them free and keeps them free (see John 8:31-32).

PROPHESY

Ask the Holy Spirit to reveal any stronghold the enemy has built in someone's life—an area where lies, fear, or sin may have taken root. Press in to discern the nature of the stronghold and how it has impacted their thoughts, emotions, or actions. Then, prophesy with boldness, exposing the enemy's scheme and declaring the truth of God's Word that dismantles it. God may lead you to prophesy freedom, victory, or a divine strategy to break the power of the stronghold and align the person's life with His purposes.

Remember, you must release this type of prophecy with great care. Don't do this randomly. Just because you see something doesn't mean you're supposed to prophesy something. God may be showing you for the sake of intercession. If you release this type of prophecy, you should do it in private if it could embarrass someone.

And this bears repeating: This exercise is not meant to expose sin but to reveal the enemy's plots and plans so someone can break through the resistance in their mind. Be careful not to make assumptions or presumptions.

ACTIVATION 48
Bring Me a Minstrel

Music can activate or enhance a prophetic atmosphere. We see this clearly in 2 Kings. Imagine the scene: Ahab was planning to go to war against the King of Moab. Before the wicked king deployed his army against the enemy, he decided to seek reinforcements. Ahab asked King Jehoshaphat to partner with him in the military campaign.

Jehoshaphat initially agreed but wanted to hear from a prophet before risking his men's lives. That's when Ahab called in his yes-men to share the "word of the Lord." A discerning Jehoshaphat wasn't quite convinced when Ahab's false prophets unanimously prophesied a sweeping victory.

Jehoshaphat wisely asked if there was "a prophet of the Lord that we may enquire of the Lord by him?" (2 Kings 3:11). When Elisha's name was mentioned, Jehoshaphat beckoned him to come. Elisha came, but wasn't excited about prophesying to his mentor Elijah's archenemy.

What happens next is telling. Elisha said, "As the Lord of hosts lives, before whom I stand, surely were it not that I regard the presence of Jehoshaphat king of Judah, I would not look at you, nor see you. But now bring me a musician." The King James Version says, "Bring me a minstrel"(2 Kings 3:14).

Elliot's Commentary for English readers suggests Elisha called for the musician to calm his perturbed spirit: "Composure and serenity of soul were essential, if the prophet was to hear the voice of God within." (There's another lesson in this: Don't prophesy when you are in your emotions.)

"Then it happened, when the anointed musician played, that the hand of the Lord came upon Elisha" (2 Kings 3:14-15). Elisha went on to prophesy a true word of the Lord, which was opposite the utterances of Ahab's false prophets—but not before getting out of his flesh and into an atmosphere that welcomed the Holy Spirit. The minstrel was the key.

Indeed, Elisha knew what I am telling you: Music can break open hard atmospheres and even shift our focus internally.

Pulpit Commentary writes, "A player on the harp seems to be intended. Music was cultivated in the schools of the prophets (1 Samuel 10:5; 1 Chronicles 25:1-3), and was employed to soothe and quiet the soul, to help it to forget things earthly and external, and bring it into that ecstatic condition in which it was most open to the reception of Divine influences."

PROPHESY

Play worship music—soft and reflective, not high praise—that helps you still your soul. Personally, I like to play the music without the words—the instrumental version.

Let the sound draw you into a place of peace. Press past your flesh and soulish distractions. It may take some time, but the right music will help create an atmosphere around you and an atmosphere in you that makes it easier hear from God.

As you enter into this receiving mode, ask the Lord to reveal His heart for someone specific. As you receive prophetic insight, allow the flow of worship and the presence of God to inspire and inform what you prophesy, releasing encouragement, hope, and life into their situation. Learn to partner with anointing that the music stirs up to enter deeper into the prophetic river.

ACTIVATION 49
Sing the Song of the Lord

When I was in Nicaragua doing missions work, a woman of God on our team prophesied in song. It was the song of the Lord. It was the first time I had ever heard anyone prophesy the song of the Lord. Indeed, we don't see this too often today—at least not beyond the worship team.

The song of the Lord is scriptural. According to *The Seer's Dictionary*, the song of the Lord is a prophetic song; Miriam released a song of the Lord in Exodus; Deborah released a song of the Lord in Judges; Zephaniah 3:14-17 is another strong example. Let's look at this passage in Zephaniah:

"Sing, O daughter of Zion! Shout, O Israel! Be glad and rejoice with all your heart, O daughter of Jerusalem! The Lord has taken away your judgments, He has cast out your enemy. The King of Israel, the Lord, is in your midst; You shall see disaster no more.

"In that day it shall be said to Jerusalem: 'Do not fear; Zion, let not your hands be weak. The Lord your God in your midst, The Mighty One, will save; He will rejoice over you with gladness, He will quiet you with His love, He will rejoice over you with singing."

The song of the Lord is not something you can plan. It's akin to what we call today "spontaneous worship" or "prophetic worship." It's not scripted. It bubbles forth, but not just in word—in song.

PROPHESY

You don't have to be an award-winning singer to release the song of the Lord. Pray over a person or people group and ask God to give you His song over them. What is God singing over someone, some group, or some nation?

You can do this privately in your own home as you are getting comfortable with the concept. Record the song of the Lord, if you can, so you can catch the spirit of what you sang. You may even want to write down the lyrics. Who knows, it could be the foundation for a song to sing in church.

ACTIVATION 50
Prophesy Inner Healing

Everyone gets hurt sometimes. We live in a fallen world with imperfect people. People we love hurt us. Strangers hurt us. Co-workers hurt us. Church members hurt us. Even when the hurt is unintentional, it can cause a great deal of pain.

The problem is hurting people hurt people, so the cycle often continues in an infinite loop. Some people easily shake off hurt and see a wound rapidly healed. Others need inner healing, often from deep-seated issues in their childhood.

Thankfully, God the Father sent Jesus to heal the brokenhearted (see Luke 4:18). And Ezekiel 36:26 tells us, "I will give you a new heart and put a new spirit within you; I will take the heart of stone out of your flesh and give you a heart of flesh." The psalmist said he "binds up" our wounds (see Psalm 147:3).

Again, it's impossible to live on this earth without getting hurt and wounded along the way. Sometimes, the wounding happens at the hand of the enemy, but usually, people cause our pain—even if the enemy is working through those people. God doesn't want us to walk around like wounded soldiers, unable to fight back against the next attack. He wants to heal our hearts.

Consider Psalm 34:18 (TPT), "The Lord is close to all whose hearts are crushed by pain, and he is always ready to restore the repentant one." And John 8:32 tells us, "And you shall know the truth, and the truth shall make you free." The reality is people cannot begin to heal until they forgive. And they need to know the truth that sets them free.

PROPHESY

Ask the Holy Spirit to reveal areas in someone's soul—mind, will, or emotions—that need healing. Take a moment to discern wounds, pain, or struggles they may be carrying, whether from traumatic experiences, betrayal, disappointment, or unmet needs.

Listen for God's truth and promises of restoration, wholeness, and peace. Prophesy with compassion, speaking directly to the areas the Holy Spirit highlights. Release His prophetic words of comfort, hope, and a revelation of God's ability to heal and restore their soul.

God may lead you to prophesy the specific restoration He has in mind. He may lead you to prophesy what happens after they forgive, or the new season He wants to bring them into, free from the pain. Get as specific as you can.

Of course, you need to do this with permission and in a private setting. It's usually inappropriate and can embarrass a person for you to call out their emotional issues publicly. I write more about these issues in my book, *Prophetic Ethics & Protocols*.

ACTIVATION 51
Prophesy Someone's Natural Inheritance

An inheritance is money or property—or something of value—that you receive from someone when they pass away. Amid the grief and pain of loss, many people receive an unexpected financial blessing. Others enter a battle in mediation—or even in court—for what is rightfully theirs according to a Last Will and Testament.

Proverbs 13:22, "A good man leaves an inheritance to his children's children, but the wealth of the sinner is stored up for the righteous." And Proverbs 19:14 says, "Houses and riches are an inheritance from fathers…" This is the will of the Lord, but it doesn't always work out that way.

In families, there are often squabbles and even lawsuits over an inheritance. In the Parable of the Rich Fool, someone from the crowd said to Jesus, "'Teacher, tell my brother to divide the inheritance with me.' But He said to him, 'Man, who made Me a judge or an arbitrator over you?' And He said to them, 'Take heed and beware of covetousness, for one's life does not consist in the abundance of the things he possesses'" (Luke 12:13-15).

We know Jacob deceived his brother Esau and stole his inheritance—the blessing that goes to the firstborn son. And David once said, "The lines have fallen to me in pleasant places; Yes, I have a good inheritance" (Psalm 16:6). Scripture is full of examples of natural inheritances.

PROPHESY

Ask the Holy Spirit to reveal insights about someone's natural inheritance—whether a blessing they are meant to receive or a battle they are facing over what was promised to them. If it's a good inheritance, prophesy details that will encourage and confirm what God has for them, highlighting His provision and plans. If there's a battle over their inheritance, listen for God's strategy for overcoming the opposition. If He tells you the outcome, prophesy the outcome.

ACTIVATION 52
Reveal Someone's Spiritual Inheritance

Although many people receive natural inheritances—some large and some small—not everyone can count on a windfall when members of their family pass away. But every person has a spiritual inheritance from their family line—sometimes that inheritance is good, and sometimes it's evil, as in the case of generational curses.

A spiritual inheritance is a divine legacy passed down from one generation to the next, rooted in God's promises, covenants, and blessings. Just as natural inheritances involve wealth, property, or heirlooms, spiritual inheritances include the mantles, gifts, wisdom, and spiritual breakthroughs God entrusts to His people to steward and pass along.

The concept of spiritual inheritance is deeply woven throughout Scripture. Consider how God promised Abraham, "And I will establish My covenant between Me and you and your descendants after you in their generations, for an everlasting covenant" (Genesis 17:7). This covenant was not just for Abraham but for all who came after him and shared in his faith.

A spiritual inheritance can manifest in several ways, including (1) Anointings and mantles: Elijah passed his prophetic mantle to Elisha, representing the double portion inheritance of his ministry (see 2 Kings 2:9-14). (2) Generational blessings: The blessings of obedience, faith, and covenant that flow through families and spiritual lineages (see Exodus 20:6). (3) Wisdom and revelation: The insights and knowledge of God that are preserved and imparted to others, as Paul told Timothy to guard the deposit entrusted to him (see 2 Timothy 1:14). (4) Spiritual Authority and Breakthrough: Victories in spiritual warfare, intimacy with God, or deliverance from strongholds that create a foundation for others to walk in freedom.

Take Philip as an example. Philip was called an evangelist and was thought to be one of the seventy Jesus sent out in Luke 10:1. He was also one of the seven original deacons handpicked to serve in the early church. I believe Philip was a prophetic evangelist, and we know he had supernatural counters, such as being transported by the spirit.

But look at this: "On the next day we who were Paul's companions departed and came to Caesarea, and entered the house of Philip the evangelist, who was one of the seven, and stayed with him. Now this man had four virgin daughters who prophesied" (Acts 21:8-9). His daughters were already partaking of the spiritual inheritance from their father.

Another example of a spiritual inheritance is Timothy and his mother. Despite his father being Greek, his mother was Jewish. Paul wrote, "For I am mindful of the sincere faith within you, which first dwelled in your grandmother Lois and your mother Eunice, and I am sure that it is in you as well" (2 Timothy 1:5, NASB).

A spiritual inheritance is not just for one person—it's meant to be passed on to the next generation. Psalm 145:4 declares, "One generation shall praise Your works to another and shall declare Your mighty acts."

PROPHESY

Ask the Lord to show you someone's spiritual inheritance. This could be someone you choose or someone the Holy Spirit highlights to you. Listen for insight into the gifts, promises, or legacy God has stored up for them.

God may lead you to prophesy what their spiritual inheritance is, as they may not yet be aware of it. He may lead you to prophesy what they need to do to activate, walk in, or guard that inheritance. Prophesy as specifically and with as much clarity as possible.

ACTIVATION 53
Reveal Someone's Inheritance in Christ

Beyond the natural and spiritual inheritances from our family line, we also have an inheritance in Christ. While some inheritances apply to us all—we are all heirs of eternal life, according to Titus 3:7—other inheritances are unique to our calling.

In Ephesians 1:11-14, Paul writes, "In Him also we have obtained an inheritance, being predestined according to the purpose of Him who works all things according to the counsel of His will, that we who first trusted in Christ should be to the praise of His glory.

"In Him you also trusted, after you heard the word of truth, the gospel of your salvation; in whom also, having believed, you were sealed with the Holy Spirit of promise, who is the guarantee of our inheritance until the redemption of the purchased possession, to the praise of His glory."

And again, Paul wrote in Ephesians 1:18, "the eyes of your understanding being enlightened; that you may know what is the hope of His calling, what are the riches of the glory of His inheritance in the saints..."

Acts 20:32 reveals, "So now, brethren, I commend you to God and to the word of His grace, which is able to build you up and give you an inheritance among all those who are sanctified."

Our ultimate inheritance in Christ is heaven. However, we don't have to wait until heaven to experience a taste of His inheritance. Jesus told His disciples how hard it is for a rich person to enter heaven. Peter spoke up about how the disciples had left everything to follow Him. Jesus replied:

"Assuredly, I say to you, there is no one who has left house or brothers or sisters or father or mother or wife or children or lands, for My sake and the gospel's, who shall not receive a hundredfold now in this time—houses and brothers and sisters and mothers and children and lands, with persecutions—and in the age to come, eternal life. But many who are first will be last, and the last first" (Mark 10:28-31)

Can you see part of heaven's best can come to a Christ-follower on earth?

PROPHESY

Ask the Lord to show you someone who needs to see and understand their inheritance in Christ. This may be a person who doesn't fully grasp who they are in Christ or the benefits of His covenant. Listen for what aspect of their inheritance God wants to highlight in this season—whether it's provision, wisdom, supernatural joy and strength, healing, deliverance, right standing with God, or authority over the enemy.

ACTIVATION 54
Expose the Obstruction

The Holy Spirit spoke expressly to me: At times, people can't see the new thing God is doing in their lives because they are mesmerized by the old thing. In other words, they are looking at the past instead of looking at the God of their future and their hope.

Isaiah prophesied, "Do not remember the former things, nor consider the things of old. Behold, I will do a new thing, now it shall spring forth; Shall you not know it? I will even make a road in the wilderness and rivers in the desert" (Isaiah 43:18-19).

Read that again. "Do not remember the former things, nor consider things of old." That's not a suggestion. That's a direct command from the Lord. When we remember the warfare, when we remember the losses, when we remember the seasons when everything that could go wrong did go wrong, we get stuck in a place called the past—a place that doesn't exist anymore.

I like the New Living Translation of this verse: "But forget all that–it is nothing compared to what I am going to do." When a person goes through a traumatic experience, it can be difficult to leave the past behind. If we meditate on the past, it can be nearly impossible to see into our future. The Holy Spirit is trying to tell and show us things to come, but the past can be an obstruction.

Sometimes, people don't know why they are stuck. But prophetic insight can help reveal the obstruction so they can face it and overtake it. One prophetic word can shed light on an old trauma the person can't even remember or open their eyes to issues in their soul that cloud their perspective.

PROPHESY

Perhaps you know someone in your life who is stuck. Maybe they don't even know they are stuck. Ask the Lord to show you what is holding them back, whether it's a victim mentality, a demon power, a lie of the enemy, grief, or something else only the Holy Spirit knows.

Handle this prophetic activation carefully and beware of words that may leave someone feeling condemned. Many times, such prophecies are better released in private—or without full details that could expose intimate matters. I write more about these issues in my book, *Prophetic Protocols & Ethics*.

ACTIVATION 55
Reveal the Hidden Things

Sometimes, the Lord hides things from us until we're ready to receive them. Remember, Jesus said this to His disciples: "I have many more things to say to you, but you cannot bear [to hear] them now" (John 16:12, AMP).

When we're not ready to hear the prophetic word, God will hold on to it until we can bear it. Sometimes, that means we have to mature a little more or get rooted a little deeper in Him. Sometimes, our faith needs to grow so we have the stamina to wage war with the prophetic word (see 1 Timothy 1:18).

But there does come a time when God will reveal the hidden things. Isaiah 48:6 tells us, "You have heard; See all this. And will you not declare it? I have made you hear new things from this time, even hidden things, and you did not know them."

The Holy Spirit is the one who reveals God's secrets over a person's life. He may reveal those things to them personally, or if they cannot hear, he could reveal them through a prophet when the person is ready to see what's been waiting in the wings. Daniel 2:22 tells us, "He reveals deep and secret things; He knows what is in the darkness, and light dwells with Him."

God knows everything and He can share with you hidden things, deep things, and secret things for the ones He loves.

PROPHESY

Wait on the Lord and ask Him to reveal a hidden blessing or purpose for someone. As you seek His guidance, listen carefully for details about what God has hidden for them—whether it's a blessing, an opportunity, or a divine strategy for breakthrough in some area of their life. Press in for as much detail as possible, seeking a clear picture of what God wants to reveal.

If you don't receive specifics, it's okay to release a more general word of encouragement, such as an exhortation from Scripture. However, challenge yourself to go deeper, pressing in for more specific insights into the hidden blessing God has purposed for the person, and prophesy with boldness.

ACTIVATION 56
Break the Generational Curse

People—yes, even Christians—can suffer the effects of a generational curse hanging over their heads. Some people never know it, while others don't believe it.

When people are hitting up against issues that seem out of their control to stop, whether it's rage, lack, infirmity, or some other problem, there could be a demon or even generational curse present.

Many times at the altar at Awakening House of Prayer, my church and house of prayer in Ft. Lauderdale, God will show me a generational curse over someone's life. Sometimes, I will call people out of the congregation and break curses. I don't always do this from the mic. I often hold the mic down and handle it privately, knowing that the congregation agrees with me and that this is the person's divine appointment for freedom.

What is a generational curse? A generational curse is a spirit that passes from generation to generation until someone finally figures out how to stop it in Jesus' name. (But in America, we don't like the word "curse.")

The world says it like this, "Like father like son." The Word says it like this, "The iniquity of the father passes on from generation to generation." Many times, we translate the word "iniquity" as "sin." But it's not the sin that passes on from generation to generation. It's the curse, the penalty.

When Jesus was walking with His disciples, they asked if the man was blind for something he did or something his parents did. Jesus didn't rebuke them for asking a foolish question because, being Jewish, they understood Ezekiel 18:2: "The fathers have eaten sour grapes, but the children's teeth are set on edge." In other words, the fathers have done something but the children pay the price.

Remember, Exodus 20:5 tells us, "You shall not bow down to them or serve them; for I, the Lord your God, am a jealous God, visiting the iniquity of the fathers on the children to the third and fourth generation of them who hate Me."

PROPHESY

If you are involved in altar ministry, deliverance ministry, or pastoral counseling, this prophetic activation is essential. Begin by practicing on yourself to ensure you are sensitive to the Holy Spirit's leading in these matters. Ask the Holy Spirit to reveal if there are any generational curses on your family line, whether they manifest in areas such as health, finances, relationships, or behavior patterns. As the Holy Spirit shows you these areas, break the curse and release God's truth over your family line.

If you are prophesying over someone else, guide them to receive freedom as you prophesy the truth that breaks the chains of generational curses. For more insight, you can refer to my course on *Deactivating Generational Curses* at www.schoolofthespirit.tv.

ACTIVATION 57
Prophesy the Transition

Everyone deals with transitions in life, and many people struggle through them in frustration, fear or some other unpleasant emotion. Transitions often bring a person to their breaking point, but many people give up and quit before they see the breakthrough.

The enemy loves to attack people in transition because they've launched out from where they were but they are not yet where God is calling them to be. Indeed, it's an opportune time for the enemy to strike.

Here's the challenge: Many believers don't discern when they are in transition. They don't understand why things are shaking or why they are getting so much warfare or why people they've walked with are leaving their lives—even with betrayal. Discouragement and self-pity are typical responses. But one prophetic word can release insight that strengthens someone to continue walking through a dry season.

Isaiah 42:9 tells us, "Behold, the former things have come to pass, and new things I declare; Before they spring forth I tell you of them." God can tell someone they are about to enter into a season of transition. He can tell them where they are in the process of transition and what to do now. He can tell them when they are about to cross the finish line. Or He can show you and you can tell them.

Think about it. When Joshua was heading into transition—leading the Israelites from the wilderness to the Promised Land—God gave him an encouraging word: "Have I not commanded you? Be strong and of good courage; do not be afraid, nor be dismayed, for the Lord your God is with you wherever you go" (Joshua 1:9).

PROPHESY

Ask the Holy Spirit to show you someone who is currently in a season of transition. Quiet your heart and let God bring a person to mind. This could be someone in the room, a friend, or even a family member.

Pray for prophetic insight about their transition. Here are some guiding questions to seek revelation: What is God doing in their transition? What is the encouragement God wants them to hear? Are there specific promises or scriptures for their season?

Write down or take note of any impressions, scriptures, images, or words you sense from the Lord. Once you have received insight, prophesy it by faith.

ACTIVATION 58
Expose an Inner Vow

Just like angels came for Daniel's words, angels come for our words—but so do demons. He comes in response to words that agree with His will. He also tempts us to make inner vows and then holds us in bondage to them when we speak them out loud, often without understanding the consequences.

Inner vows are promises we make to ourselves, usually in reaction to emotional pain, trauma, or something that angers us. We're saying, "God, if you can't, then I will." We are trying to guard and protect ourselves, but we're unwittingly inviting demons to guard us. We're signing a contract with the enemy.

Jesus said in Matthew 5:34-35. "But I say to you, do not swear at all: neither by heaven, for it is God's throne; nor by the earth, for it is His footstool; nor by Jerusalem, for it is the city of the great King. Nor shall you swear by your head, because you cannot make one hair white or black. But let your 'Yes' mean 'Yes,' and 'No' mean 'No.' For whatever is more than these comes from the evil one."

People often make inner vows as children or during times of great stress or crisis as adults. They may forget all about the words they uttered, but the vow is nevertheless intact. Remember, Jesus said in Matthew 12:36-37, "I say to you that for every idle word men may speak, they will give account of it in the day of judgment. For by your words you will be justified, and by your words you will be condemned."

You may hear people reciting their inner vows when they make "I will never" or "I always" statements. But the Holy Spirit can also show them—or you—that an inner vow is present. Prophesying to expose an inner vow over a person so that it can be broken can is a transformative act of love.

PROPHESY

Ask the Holy Spirit to reveal any inner vow someone has made that is hindering their freedom or growth. These could be statements they've made in pain, fear, or self-protection, such as, "I'll never trust anyone again" or "I'm not good enough."

Listen for God's insight into how this vow specifically affected their lives and relationships. Prophesy to expose the lie behind the vow and declare God's truth that breaks its power. God may also lead you to prophesy the freedom, healing, and alignment with His will that will come after the vow is broken.

ACTIVATION 59
After You Prophesy

Prophetic ministry puts a strong demand on your soul and body. After all, you must crucify your flesh to maintain sensitivity to the Spirit. You have to cultivate a listening ear. You have to learn to judge your prophetic words before you release them, especially if they move beyond edification, exhortation, and comfort. You have to release the word with confidence, and sometimes, you have to endure retaliation from the enemy in the form of persecution or spiritual warfare.

After you prophesy, it's important that you cool down. Think of it like running a race or exercising with heavy weights. When you exercise, there's a warm-up and a cool-down (or at least there should be!). Your warm-up might be praying in tongues, or worshipping the Lord in Spirit and truth, or reading Scripture, or meditating on Scripture or gazing upon the beauty of the Lord. But what about the cool down? How do you restore yourself after extensive prophetic ministry?

I was struck by what Samuel wrote about Saul. Saul started prophesying after he came upon a company of prophets. Apparently, he was so accurate and prolific that those standing around said, "Can anyone become a prophet, no matter who his father is?' So that is the origin of the saying "Is even Saul a prophet?" (1 Samuel 10:12, NLT).

I am sure Saul was taken aback. He may have been physically tired. His soul may have had questions. What did he do? Go get a cheeseburger to feed his flesh? No, "When Saul had finished prophesying, he went up to the place of worship" (1 Samuel 10:13, NLT).

Wow! He went to the place of worship. He worshiped the one who gave Him the words to prophesy. He went to pour his heart out to the God who gave him the unction to function. In doing so, he got refilled for his assignment. So can you! Maybe your cool down isn't worship. Maybe it's physical rest, refilling with the Word, or something unique to your relationship with Him.

REFRESH

After you have prophesied, it's essential to take time to refuel and refill in His presence. Ministry can drain you, but God faithfully replenishes what has been poured out. Begin by taking a moment to pause and reflect on the word you released, thanking God for the opportunity to be His mouthpiece.

Invite the Holy Spirit to strengthen you, asking for a fresh infilling of His power, wisdom, and joy. Spend time in worship, prayer, or the Word to reconnect with God's heart and allow Him to restore your energy and spiritual strength. Like a vessel that needs to be refilled, allow God to pour back into you what you've given out.

As you soak in His presence, trust that He will refresh you and fill you with renewed vision, strength, and grace to continue His work. Remember, you are not meant to minister in your own strength but to operate out of His supernatural grace.

ACTIVATION 60
Prophesy in a Group

At our Elijah Company intensives, the atmosphere is supercharged with the spirit of prophecy. That's because it's not just my mantle—and the mantle of house prophets—in the building. Prophets and highly prophetic people also bring their anointing with them.

The result? People step into new realms. dimensions and levels they have never before experienced This is what can happen when you prophesy in a group.

Indeed, this was Saul's experience—and it wasn't a fluke. Saul experienced this not once but twice, demonstrating a spiritual principle. (This also happened in 1 Samuel 10). 1 Samuel 19:19-21 reads:

"Now it was told Saul, saying, 'Take note, David is at Naioth in Ramah!' Then Saul sent messengers to take David. And when they saw the group of prophets prophesying, and Samuel standing as leader over them, the Spirit of God came upon the messengers of Saul, and they also prophesied. And when Saul was told, he sent other messengers, and they prophesied likewise. Then Saul sent messengers again the third time, and they prophesied also."

It's powerful to find a group of prophetic people to minister with—or even to practice with. Just as one can put a thousand to flight and two can put ten thousand to flight, prophetic synergy is released when there are groups of prophets.

PROPHESY

Gather with a group of believers, creating an atmosphere of unity and expectation. Begin by inviting the Holy Spirit to lead and fill the group, asking God to speak through each of you. As you wait on the Lord, listen for any specific words of encouragement, revelation, or insight He may want to release to the group.

Start by prophesying a word to one person in the group. God may lead you to release a word of encouragement, prophetic direction, or His solution to their current problem. Encourage others in the group to also share what they are hearing from the Lord.

End by thanking God for what He has spoken, and ask for continued clarity and vision as you move forward together as a company of prophets.

ACTIVATION 61
Prophesying in the Face of Resistance

The higher you ascend in the prophetic, the more resistance you will have from demons and people alike. Let's focus right now on the people part of the equation, taking a page from Micaiah's experience with King Ahab.

In 1 Kings 22, we find peace in the land. Judah's King Jehoshaphat went down to visit Ahab, and they discussed taking Gilead out of the hand of Syria. Ahab gathered all his yes men to get "prophetic direction." Of course, they all falsely prophesied an overwhelming victory. These were Ahab's yes-men. They told the king whatever he wanted to hear to continue currying his favor.

"And Jehoshaphat said, 'Is there not still a prophet of the Lord here, that we may inquire of Him?' So the king of Israel said to Jehoshaphat, 'There is still one man, Micaiah the son of Imlah, by whom we may inquire of the Lord; but I hate him, because he does not prophesy good concerning me, but evil.' And Jehoshaphat said, 'Let not the king say such things!' Then the king of Israel called an officer and said, 'Bring Micaiah the son of Imlah quickly!'" (1 Kings 22:7-9)

Micaiah had to prophesy the opposite of what Ahab wanted to hear. He knew the risk was real. Yet Micaiah was bold enough not to compromise the word of the Lord to pump up the ego of a corrupt king. He ended up being put in prison. But Ahab ended up dead. Determine to prophesy in the face of resistance—whether internal or external.

PROPHESY

Ask the Holy Spirit to reveal an area where you are feeling resistance in releasing a prophetic word—such as fear, doubt, or opposition from others. Recognize that resistance often comes when you're on the verge of breaking through and releasing God's truth. Take a moment to reflect on how prophets, like Micaiah in 1 Kings 22, faced resistance but remained faithful to speak God's word despite the pressure—or the potential consequences.

Pray for the courage to speak the word of the Lord with boldness, even when fear or doubt tries to hold you back—or people or demons are silently or openly resisting you. Ask God to give you a forehead like flint to stand firm, trusting His word will accomplish its purpose no matter the opposition.

Determine in your heart that the resistance will not stop the flow of God's prophetic word. Begin to speak the prophetic word out loud, even if it feels difficult. Push through any external opposition, knowing God's truth is stronger than any resistance. Trust that as you continue to speak, God's power will break through and His word will accomplish what He desires.

ACTIVATION 62
Prophesy on an Instrument

We've heard of prophetic songs, but just because you can't sing doesn't mean you can't prophesy musically. If you are a musician, you can prophesy on your instrument. This is what we see in 1 Chronicles 25:1-3:

"Moreover David and the captains of the army separated for the service some of the sons of Asaph, of Heman, and of Jeduthun, who should prophesy with harps, stringed instruments, and cymbals. And the number of the skilled men performing their service was:

"Of the sons of Asaph: Zaccur, Joseph, Nethaniah, and Asharelah; the sons of Asaph were under the direction of Asaph, who prophesied according to the order of the king. Of Jeduthun, the sons of Jeduthun: Gedaliah, Zeri, Jeshaiah, Shimei, Hashabiah, and Mattithiah, six, under the direction of their father Jeduthun, who prophesied with a harp to give thanks and to praise the Lord."

Catch that: He prophesied with a harp. What does prophesying on an instrument mean? It's creating a new song, a new sound on the guitar, the drums, the keys, or some other apparatus.

Prophesying on the instrument is releasing the sound of heaven into an atmosphere, with or without words. It's issuing harmonies and melodies that align with the grace God is releasing. If you are a musician, prophesy on your instrument.

PROPHESY

Pick up your instrument and take a moment to quiet your heart, inviting the Holy Spirit to guide you. Ask God to speak through your music, trusting that your instrument can carry prophetic messages without words.

Begin playing softly, listening for the melodies and rhythms the Holy Spirit places on your heart. Allow the sound to flow freely, and as you play, prophesy through the notes.

Don't worry about the technicality of the music; focus instead on releasing what the Holy Spirit is prompting you to play. Each note, chord, or melody can carry the weight of God's encouragement, healing, or grace needed in the moment. As you do, be confident that your instrument is a prophetic tool—God can communicate through the music itself, bringing peace, breakthrough, or awakening.

As you continue to play, listen for any images, impressions, or words that may arise within you and prophesy them. Even if you don't hear or say anything, know your music is prophesying, releasing what God desires to communicate to someone's heart. Play with faith, knowing that your instrument is a vessel for His voice, and allow it to become an extension of the prophetic ministry.

ACTIVATION 63
Prophesy Against What the Lord Hates

I prophesy against things at the Holy Spirit's leading. What does that mean? God will lead me to prophesy against nuclear war, for example, or prophesy against corruption.

Prophesying against something usually has elements such as calling out something the Lord doesn't like, issuing a warning, or rooting out, tearing down, throwing down, and destroying through prophecy. It can also be a word of correction. I've prophesied against evil regimes, for example, and against evil practices that stand against the Lord and His Gospel.

Hosea prophesied against the Israelites. It was a word of correction. Notice how the words are metaphorical. Hosea 6:5-10 offers:

"I sent my prophets to cut you to pieces—to slaughter you with my words, with judgments as inescapable as light. I want you to show love, not offer sacrifices. I want you to know me more than I want burnt offerings. But like Adam, you broke my covenant and betrayed my trust.

"Gilead is a city of sinners, tracked with footprints of blood. Priests form bands of robbers, waiting in ambush for their victims. They murder travelers along the road to Shechem and practice every kind of sin. Yes, I have seen something horrible in Ephraim and Israel: My people are defiled by prostituting themselves with other gods!"

When you prophesy against what the Lord hates, you must double down on judging the words and motives of your heart. You need to check your biases. Some prophets unwittingly prophesy a curse or judgment when the Lord has not spoken.

PROPHESY

Ask the Holy Spirit to reveal areas where God's heart is grieved or where the enemy has established strongholds that align with what the Lord hates. These could be areas of sin, injustice, idolatry, division, pride, or oppression. Reflect on what Scripture says God despises (Proverbs 6:16-19 lists things the Lord hates, such as pride, lying, and strife).

As you press into God's heart, ask Him to give you discernment to identify these areas. Once you have clarity, prophesy with boldness against these things. Speak with the authority of Christ the Prophet. He may lead you to decree that every stronghold tied to what the Lord hates is being uprooted. Command these forces to be broken and bind them in the name of Jesus.

But don't stop there. Declare the establishment of God's righteousness, peace, and justice in place of the evil works. Speak life, truth, and restoration over the areas where sin or opposition has taken root. Declare that God's will is being done, and His kingdom is advancing, overcoming every work of the enemy. Prophesy with confidence, knowing that God's Word is more powerful than any resistance, and His plans will ultimately prevail.

ACTIVATION 64
Prophesy What Not to Do

As part of directional prophecy (and sometimes part of the warning realm or corrective realm of prophecy), God sometimes instructs people what not to do. We see this in Scripture.

Isaiah prophesied, "Do not remember the former things, nor consider the things of old. Behold, I will do a new thing, now it shall spring forth; Shall you not know it?" (Isaiah 43:18-19). Isaiah's utterance was a prophetic encouragement not to look at the past but to press into the future and hope. So the prophet didn't just tell people what to do, but also what not to do.

Again, Isaiah 8:12 prophesies, "Do not say, 'A conspiracy,' Concerning all that this people call a conspiracy, Nor be afraid of their threats, nor be troubled." This was a word of warning not to get caught up in the ways of the world.

God prophesied to Jeremiah, "'Do not say, 'I am a youth,' For you shall go to all to whom I send you, And whatever I command you, you shall speak" (Jeremiah 1:7). This was God making sure Jeremiah was not going to let people intimidate or disqualify him because of his age. There are many "do not" prophecies throughout Scripture.

God uses "do not" prophecies to wake us up, to warn us about entangling ourselves with people, or to encourage our hearts not to fear, and so on.

PROPHESY

Ask the Holy Spirit to bring to mind someone facing a decision or situation needing guidance. As you wait on the Lord, ask Him to reveal any actions, paths, or behaviors that He would caution them against. This could be, for example, a situation in which they may be tempted to make a choice that doesn't align with God's will.

Once you sense God's direction, prophesy with clarity about what not to do. God may lead you to prophetically urge them to avoid the wrong paths, actions, or mindsets that may lead to harm, confusion, or delay. God may lead you to prophesy pitfalls or traps.

With your delivery, be gentle but firm. Trust that as you prophesy what not to do, the Holy Spirit will bring conviction and clarity to help them make wise choices that align with God's will.

ACTIVATION 65
Prophesy on Location

There's something about prophesying on location. Although there's no distance in the spirit, God will sometimes send you to a specific location to prophesy with boots on the ground. God has assigned me to the Berlin Wall, the city streets, and many other places. He sent Amos to prophesy on location as well.

We see this in Amos 7:14-16. Amos said to Amaziah: "I was no prophet, nor was I a son of a prophet, but I was a sheepbreeder and a tender of sycamore fruit. Then the Lord took me as I followed the flock, and the Lord said to me, 'Go, prophesy to My people Israel.' Now therefore, hear the word of the Lord: You say, 'Do not prophesy against Israel, and do not spout against the house of Isaac.'"

Notice how the Lord didn't tell him to stand where he was and prophesy. God said, "Go prophesy." This was part of Amos' commissioning. He didn't consider himself a prophet. He saw himself as a sheep breeder, which was his natural trade. But suddenly, God gave him an assignment to "go prophesy." Amos couldn't stay there in the fields and prophesy. He had to leave that place and go to another place to fulfill his spiritual assignment.

Specifically, Amos had to leave the land of Judah, which was probably all he knew, to obey the call. At times, you can't just prophesy in your house or prophesy within the four walls of the church. God will send you to a place to prophesy into the atmosphere.

PROPHESY

Ask the Holy Spirit to lead you to a specific location, whether it's a place in your city, a region, or even a specific room or building. Take time to listen and be sensitive to the atmosphere around you. Ask God to reveal His heart for that location and any prophetic words He wants to release.

Release prophetic words that align with God's plan for that location. He may lead you to call forth the potential He sees in it. Know that as you prophesy on location, the environment will shift and align with God's Kingdom purposes, and that your words will have a lasting impact.

Alternatively, you can ask God for a prophetic word for a particular pace and then go to that place to prophesy. Practically speaking, this needs to be somewhere local, such as a park, an airport, a courthouse or some other physical location you can easily get to.

ACTIVATION 66
Share the Next Step

God orders our steps, therefore He knows what the next step—and steps—are. Psalm 37:23 makes this clear: "The steps of a good man are ordered by the Lord, and He delights in his way." And again, Psalm 32:8 makes this clear: "I will instruct you and teach you in the way you should go; I will guide you with My eye."

Sometimes, people can't see their next step. They feel stuck and hopeless. Prophesying the next step sparks faith in someone's heart. Other times, people think they know what the next step is but are scared they may not be discerning correctly. In those cases, prophesying the next step can bring confirmation.

Isaiah prophesied, "Your ears shall hear a word behind you, saying, 'This is the way, walk in it,' whenever you turn to the right hand or whenever you turn to the left" (Isaiah 30:21). Sometimes the Lord is trying to show someone what the next steps are but the enemy is clouding their mind. Prophesying the next step can bring clarity where confusion exists.

Sometimes, people know what the next step is but need to be encouraged that God will provide the people, finances, and other resources along the way. Prophesying the next step can assure them that God is in it with them. God prophesied to Joshua, "Have I not commanded you? Be strong and of good courage; do not be afraid, nor be dismayed, for the Lord your God is with you wherever you go" (Joshua 1:9).

PROPHESY

Ask the Holy Spirit to bring to mind someone who is seeking direction or is at a crossroads in their life. Spend a moment in prayer, asking God to reveal the next step He wants them to take, whether in their career, relationships, ministry, or personal life.

Once you feel you have received the direction, begin to prophesy the next step with as much specificity as possible. God may lead you to prophesy a word of encouragement, wisdom, or direction. If the person is dealing with hesitation or fear, God may lead you to prophesy courage and boldness to take that step.

God may lead you to encourage them to trust in His timing, knowing He will make the path clear. Or He may lead you to prophesy the breakthrough that comes when they take that next step.

ACTIVATION 67
When God Asks Questions

Sometimes, when I prophesy, God will ask a question in the midst of the prophecy. Know this: God doesn't ask questions because He doesn't know the answer.

Sometimes, He's trying to get you—or the person to whom you are prophesying—to ponder a thing. Sometimes, He's trying to point someone's attention to a thing. Sometimes, He's trying to remind someone of something He said in the past or promised for the future. Then again, sometimes the question is rhetorical, which means it's a question asked in order to make a point rather than to get an answer.

God spoke to Adam and asked, "Where are you?" God knew where Adam was, but He demonstrated to Adam that there was a disconnect. God spoke to Moses and asked, "What's in your hand? God knew what was in Moses' hand, but wanted to emphasize this point of contact with the supernatural.

God asked Joshua, "Have I not commanded you? Be strong and courageous, be not afraid, neither be you dismayed…" (Joshua 1:9). God reminded Joshua of what He had already said to encourage Him.

God said through Isaiah, "Do not remember the former things, Nor consider the things of old. Behold, I will do a new thing, Now it shall spring forth; Shall you not know it?" (Isaiah 43:18-19). This was God making a promise and a call to watch for the new thing.

God asked the Israelites, "Is it time for you yourselves to dwell in your paneled houses, and this temple to lie in ruins?" Now therefore, thus says the Lord of hosts: 'Consider your ways!'" (Haggai 1:4-5). This question was convicting and correcting.

PROPHESY

Ask the Holy Spirit to show you someone who needs a prophetic word and to reveal if there are any questions God wants to ask them as part of the word.

Once you have someone in mind, begin to pray and wait on the Lord for His direction. Listen carefully for any questions the Holy Spirit places on your heart. These questions could be personal, relational, or about a specific situation. Remember, questions from God are not for His information. Rather, they are often meant to awaken understanding, serve as an important reminder, spark repentance, or give someone a new perspective.

After you release your prophecy with God's question, ask the person to reflect on it. It's important that they sit with the Lord and think on these things.

ACTIVATION 68
Prophesy the Sound

After the showdown at Mt. Carmel that saw Israel turn back to God, Elijah told King Ahab: "Go up, eat and drink; for there is the sound of abundance of rain" (1 Kings 18:41).

Elijah issued this command after he heard the sound of the abundance of rain. But consider this: Elijah heard the sound of rain in the spirit realm, not the natural realm. We know this because after he exhorted Ahab, he prayed a long time before finally seeing a cloud the size of a man's hand in the sky.

Deeply ponder this: Elijah heard the sound of rain in the spirit before he saw the manifestation of rain in the natural.

God didn't create the world in silence. Genesis leaves us with a detailed record of how He created the world—and everything in it. God created with the sound of His voice.

Likewise, heaven is full of sounds, from angels rejoicing over lost souls coming to salvation to the four living creatures crying "holy, holy, holy," to thunderings and lightnings around the throne. The world is full of sounds we hear and don't hear, including ultrasonic and subsonic sound waves.

Clearly, God values sound—and God Himself sings (see Zephaniah 3:17). Sound existed before Adam. Angels were praising God in heaven before the earth was formed. Lucifer was making music before his fall (Ezekiel 28:12-12).

The sons of God shouted for joy after God laid the earth's foundations—before mankind ever was (see Job 38:7). Sound is so important to creation that God created sound before He created man, the seas, the plants, and the animals. That's something!

God created everything with the sound of His words. He uses sound to communicate with mankind and to enable mankind—and animals—to communicate with each other. We should appreciate sound because God created it. When we appreciate something, we recognize its value. When we recognize the value of something, we pay attention to it. When we pay attention to something, we can reap greater rewards from it.

PROPHESY

Take a moment to quiet your heart and invite the Holy Spirit to open your spiritual ears. Ask God to let you hear a sound in the spirit, whether it's something unfamiliar or a familiar sound with a deeper meaning. Pay close attention to what you hear.

Once you hear the sound, ask God what that sound is, especially if it's unfamiliar to you. Ask God what the sound signifies and how it connects to the prophetic word He wants to release.

Prophesy based on the sound you heard and the revelation you received about its meaning. If you don't know the meaning of the sound, prophesy what you heard anyway, as it should have meaning to the person you are prophesying to. After all, the sound wasn't for you. It was for them.

ACTIVATION 69
Prophesy to the Wind

In the context of the valley of the dry bones, God gave Ezekiel a strange command: Prophesy to the wind.

"Then said he unto me, 'Prophesy unto the wind, prophesy, son of man, and say to the wind, Thus saith the Lord God; Come from the four winds, O breath, and breathe upon these slain, that they may live'" (Ezekiel 37:9, KJV).

The New Living Translation says, "Speak a prophetic message to the winds, son of man. Speak a prophetic message and say, 'This is what the Sovereign Lord says: Come, O breath, from the four winds! Breathe into these dead bodies so they may live again.'"

What does it mean to prophesy to the wind? Theologians have slightly differing views, but when we see the results of Ezekiel's prophecy it leaves little question that this speaks of dead things coming to life—and not just coming to life but coming to life with strength and vigor.

Wind is a symbol of the Holy Spirit. Jesus told Nicodemus, "The wind blows where it wishes, and you hear the sound of it, but cannot tell where it comes from and where it goes. So is everyone who is born of the Spirit" (John 3:8).

When Ezekiel prophesied to the winds, "breath came into them, and they lived, and stood upon their feet, an exceedingly great army" (Ez. 37:10). The result of prophesying to the winds was life-giving power that revived what seemed lost.

PROPHESY

Sometimes people don't even know they need revival, and other times they do. Ask the Holy Spirit to show you something in a person's life that needs the breath of God to bring revival and restoration. It could be an area of their heart, a relationship, a dream, or a ministry that has grown dry or stagnant. Allow the Holy Spirit to give you insight into where His breath is needed.

As you receive this revelation, begin to prophesy to the wind, just as Ezekiel did. God may lead you to prophesy to the wind to restore a dry place in their marriage, finances or career. Remember, it doesn't have to make sense to your natural mind.

ACTIVATION 70
Keeping Prophetic Receipts

When you own a business, you must keep receipts of your expenses, such as office supplies, travel, and mileage. It's wise to keep receipts in your prophetic ministry as well.

Keeping receipts is another way to say, "showing proof." This is often done through a wrong spirit by people who want to tell the world how accurate they are. If that is your motive, it's called self-exaltation. Solomon offered these wise words for such people: "Let another man praise you, and not your own mouth; A stranger, and not your own lips" (Proverbs 27:2).

However, there is a right motive for keeping receipts. It can help you develop confidence in your prophetic gifting. You should keep receipts to encourage yourself. You can also keep receipts to encourage other people, such as intercessors who took your prophetic word and warred with it until it came to pass or stopped an enemy attack because of the prophetic warning.

In other words, when you prophesied with a charge to intercessors to stand in the gap over a matter and the victory comes, remind them how their faithful stance on the wall made all the difference. This will encourage them to keep warring with the prophetic words you and others release.

When you set out to keep receipts, though, you should also track when you need to give a refund. In other words, if we are going to track when we are right, we also need to track when we are wrong. Otherwise, we're not being responsible with our gifting. It's poor prophetic character.

Remember, you aren't keeping receipts to flaunt your accuracy on social media. We see far too much of that. Paul warned, "When people commend themselves, it doesn't count for much. The important thing is for the Lord to commend them" (see 2 Corinthians 10:18). We are keeping receipts, like a business owner who's accountable to the IRS, to responsibly learn and grow and help others do the same.

REFLECTION

Start by thinking about the prophetic words you've released over others—whether it's been encouragement, guidance, or direction. Take time to record these words, noting the specific details, dates, and context of each prophecy. Writing them down will help you maintain a clear record and allow you to revisit them later to see how they have been fulfilled or are still in progress.

Ask the Holy Spirit to reveal any confirmations or fruit that has come from the prophetic words you've released—or better yet ask the person if you can. Also ask Him to show you times you missed it, and ask Him how you missed it.

Keeping prophetic receipts helps build confidence in hearing and releasing God's voice. It also provides an opportunity to track His faithfulness, seeing how He works through your words. Review your prophetic receipts regularly, as they will encourage you to step out in faith and prophesy with greater accuracy, knowing that God is faithful to bring His words to pass.

Start making a habit of writing down significant prophecies the Holy Spirit has given you about people, places or things. And always hold yourself accountable for your misses. That's part of how you build prophetic integrity.

ACTIVATION 71
Commanded Not to Prophesy

In the modern-day prophetic movement, prophets are all too ready to prophesy. It's wonderful to see people edified, comforted, and exhorted. But there are times when people refuse to let you prophesy—and if God is the one putting the words in your mouth, He doesn't take too kindly to people quenching His Spirit at work through you.

Such was the case in the story of Amos. Amos was a farmer, and God called him into prophetic ministry. Suddenly, he found himself standing in the office of the prophet and had the uncomfortable task of prophesying judgment. In Amos 2, he prophesied judgment against Moab, Kerioth, Judah, and all of Israel. As part of that string of judgments, we read something interesting in Amos 2:11-12:

"I raised up some of your sons as prophets, and some of your young men as Nazirites. Is it not so, O you children of Israel?" says the Lord. "But you gave the Nazirites wine to drink, and commanded the prophets saying, 'Do not prophesy!'"

Israel was rejecting the prophetic voice of God. God had commanded the prophets to prophesy, but the people did not want to hear the word of the Lord. Essentially, the prophetic word was forbidden. The people did not want to hear the warnings of the Lord. They only wanted smooth sayings. As a result of rejecting the prophets who carried the word of the Lord, judgment fell.

PROPHESY

Take a moment to reflect on times when you have been rejected in your prophetic ministry or when you have been commanded not to speak. Understand that rejection of prophetic words does not diminish their truth or value. In times like these, God is still working in the hearts of those who hear, even if they don't receive it immediately. Remember, your responsibility is to speak the word He has given you.

Ask the Holy Spirit to help you work through any discouragement or frustration that might arise from rejection. If you have been commanded not to prophesy or your words have been rejected, choose to pray for those who have turned away. Ask God to open their hearts to His truth and to bring conviction and healing.

Release any self-pity or discouragement, knowing that when you speak accurately, you have done your part. Trust that the seed has been planted, and in due time, it will bear fruit. Rejoice in the knowledge that you are being faithful to what God has called you to do.

Pray that they would receive the word of the Lord in His timing, and that their hearts would be softened to His will. Even if they don't want to hear it now, God's word will not return void (Isaiah 55:11).

ACTIVATION 72
Prophesy a Provision Strategy

God is not just a provider—He's our provider. Paul reminds us, "But my God shall supply all your need according to his riches in glory by Christ Jesus" (Philippians 4:19).

We see God providing miraculously through the pages of Scripture. In the wilderness, God brought water from a rock and caused quail and manna to fall from the sky. Jesus fed thousands of people with a few fish and loaves—twice! Elisha blessed twenty barely loves during a time of famine, and God multiplied it enough to feed one hundred people, with scraps left over. Jesus also made a miraculous provision for His and Peter's taxes.

But Elijah prophesied a provision strategy. We find it in 1 Kings 17. The brook dried up, and God told Elijah to see a widow in Zarephath who would meet his needs. Elijah obeyed the Lord, found the widow was gathering sticks, and asked her to bring him some water and bread.

The widow protested, telling Elijah she had no bread—only a handful of flour in a bin and a little oil in a jar. She planned to cook it, eat it and die. 1 Kings 17:13-16 reads:

"And Elijah said to her, 'Do not fear; go and do as you have said, but make me a small cake from it first, and bring it to me; and afterward make some for yourself and your son. For thus says the Lord God of Israel: 'The bin of flour shall not be used up, nor shall the jar of oil run dry, until the day the Lord sends rain on the earth.'"

"So she went away and did according to the word of Elijah; and she and he and her household ate for many days. The bin of flour was not used up, nor did the jar of oil run dry, according to the word of the Lord which He spoke by Elijah."

PROPHESY

Ask the Holy Spirit to reveal to you the provision strategy that He has for you or someone else. What does God want to reveal about your finances, your job, your ministry, or your resources? Are there new opportunities, new streams, or areas where God wants to open doors?

Begin by prophesying over your own situation, speaking God's promises of provision over every area of your life. Ask God to show you what actions to take, what doors to knock on, and where to sow.

You can also prophesy a provision strategy over someone else. God may lead you to prophesy new revenue streams, new business ideas, wisdom, favor or opportunities. God may lead you to prophesy against barriers to financial breakthrough.

ACTIVATION 73
Ask God for an End-Times Word

The signs of the times are all around us. It doesn't take a prophet to see that Christ's prophecies in Matthew 24 are coming to pass before our eyes. Although the scenes in the Book of Revelation have not yet manifested as of the time of this writing, we are well on our way to seeing even more shocking events on earth.

Read and meditate on the words of Christ in Matthew 24:4-13 and ask God to give you a word about the end times. It could be a warning or a word of preparation or encouragement. Jesus said:

"Take heed that no one deceives you. For many will come in My name, saying, 'I am the Christ,' and will deceive many. And you will hear of wars and rumors of wars. See that you are not troubled; for all these things must come to pass, but the end is not yet. For nation will rise against nation, and kingdom against kingdom. And there will be famines, pestilences, and earthquakes in various places. All these are the beginning of sorrows.

"Then they will deliver you up to tribulation and kill you, and you will be hated by all nations for My name's sake. And then many will be offended, will betray one another, and will hate one another. Then many false prophets will rise up and deceive many. And because lawlessness will abound, the love of many will grow cold. But he who endures to the end shall be saved. And this gospel of the kingdom will be preached in all the world as a witness to all the nations, and then the end will come."

PROPHESY

The Holy Spirit is always speaking, and these days, He is revealing more of the Father's plans and purposes for the end times. Take a moment to come before the Lord and ask Him for a prophetic word about what He is doing in this season as it relates to the last days. God wants to prepare His people, and He may give you specific strategies for both spiritual and natural preparation.

Ask God to reveal His heart for the end times. What is He showing you about the current spiritual climate? What is He calling the Church to do in these last days? Pray for discernment as you listen for His voice. God may speak through Scripture, visions, dreams, or a still small voice, but be open to receiving from Him in any way He chooses.

As you wait on the Lord, allow His Word to stir you to action. The end times are not meant to bring fear but to ignite faith that Jesus is coming soon. God has a plan for His people, and He desires to use you in this critical moment. Prophesy what you hear, whether it's a word of encouragement, a call to repentance, or a divine strategy for the Church in the coming days.

Commit to staying alert and receptive to God's voice, knowing He will continue to guide you and reveal His plans as you seek Him. Keep your heart aligned with His purposes, and trust that the Holy Spirit will equip you with the wisdom and boldness needed to fulfill your calling in these last days.

ACTIVATION 74
Reveal the Ways of the Lord

Prophets are called to make straight the way of the Lord (see John 1:23). That speaks to preparing the Bride for His Second Coming, but we can also apply this to prophesying the way of the Lord in someone's life.

God makes His ways known to prophets so they can make His ways known to the people. Consider Psalm 103:7, "He made known His ways to Moses." This, of course, was after Moses asked the Lord, "Now therefore, I pray, if I have found grace in Your sight, show me now Your way, that I may know You and that I may find grace in Your sight" (see Exodus 33:13).

David, another prophet, also desires to know God's ways. His cry, "Teach me Your way, O Lord" (Psalm 86:11). And again, "Show me Your ways, O Lord; Teach me Your paths" (Psalm 25:4). David desired to meditate on God's precepts and regard His ways (see Psalm 119:26).

As prophets and prophetic people, we should get beyond ourselves and prophesy the Lord's ways to others. Perhaps they are walking through a trial; what is God's way for them to handle it? Maybe it's an intense season of spiritual warfare. In what way would God lead them to battle back? It could be sudden prosperity or grief. What is God's way to move through those seasons?

Isaiah prophesied, "For My thoughts are not your thoughts, nor are your ways My ways," says the Lord. "For as the heavens are higher than the earth, so are My ways higher than your ways, and My thoughts than your thoughts" (Isaiah 55:8-9). God's way is perfect and He has a way for us to walk in. God is the way, the truth and the life.

PROPHESY

Begin by asking the Holy Spirit to reveal the specific situation God wants to address. This could be someone you know or someone God highlights to you in prayer. Once God has brought their situation to your heart, ask Him to show you His ways in that situation—how He wants to move, what He wants to release, and the steps He is calling them to take. Prophesy what you hear. For example, God may lead you to prophesy that His ways will prevail over confusion, that His wisdom will lead the way, and that His will shall be done.

ACTIVATION 75
Release a Word Without Speaking

Francis of Assisi once said, "Preach the gospel at all times and if necessary, use words." Did you know you can prophesy without speaking a word? Most people have not considered this. Let's look at the story of Elijah and Elisha.

After a fierce battle with the prophets of Baal and a death curse from Jezebel that sent Elijah running to hide in a cave, God told Elijah to anoint Elisha as prophet in his place. 1 Kings 19:19-20 reads:

"So he departed from there, and found Elisha the son of Shaphat, who was plowing with twelve yoke of oxen before him, and he was with the twelfth. Then Elijah passed by him and threw his mantle on him. And he left the oxen and ran after Elijah, and said, 'Please let me kiss my father and my mother, and then I will follow you'."

Elijah didn't have to say a word, but Elisha knew the elder prophet was prophesying his calling. This was a prophetic act. A prophetic act is a nonverbal action that communicates a message. Prophetic acts can speak volumes in much the same way as a picture can speak a thousand words.

A prophetic act in modern times might look like going to a high point in a city and waving a flag in worship to the Lord. It may look like walking seven times around a government building or standing in front of an abortion clinic with tape on your mouth. A prophetic act may look like sprinkling salt in a river to cleanse it.

The prophet Elisha joined a king in a prophetic act in 2 Kings 13:15-19: "And Elisha said to him, 'Take a bow and some arrows.' So he took himself a bow and some arrows. Then he said to the king of Israel, 'Put your hand on the bow.' So he put his hand on it, and Elisha put his hands on the king's hands. And he said, 'Open the east window"; and he opened it. Then Elisha said, 'Shoot'; and he shot. And he said, 'The arrow of the Lord's deliverance and the arrow of deliverance from Syria; for you must strike the Syrians at Aphek till you have destroyed them.'

"Then he said, 'Take the arrows'; so he took them. And he said to the king of Israel, 'Strike the ground'; so he struck three times, and stopped. And the man of God was angry with him, and said, 'You should have struck five or six times; then you would have struck Syria till you had destroyed it! But now you will strike Syria only three times."

PROPHESY

Ask the Holy Spirit if there is a situation or person where He wants to speak without words. Be still and open your heart to His direction. You may feel prompted to lay hands on someone in prayer, to stand in a specific posture, or even to engage in a prophetic act like walking or writing something out.

As you begin, trust that your body is a vessel for God's prophetic message. Maybe He will guide you to extend a hand to someone in a symbolic gesture of blessing or raise your hands in an act of surrender. If you are led to perform a prophetic act, do it with full faith, knowing that even though you aren't speaking, you are releasing a powerful word through your actions.

When you step into a prophetic act, you are releasing heaven's purposes into the earth. Be confident that God can speak through you in any way He chooses—even without words.

ACTIVATION 76
Prophesy the Blessing from the Curse

God can turn a curse into a blessing. When Absalom launched an insurrection in Jerusalem, David left barefoot and weeping. Adding insult to injury, Shimei cursed him. David understood that God can turn the curse into a blessing, saying:

"Let him alone, and let him curse; for so the Lord has ordered him. It may be that the Lord will look on my affliction, and that the Lord will repay me with good for his cursing this day" (2 Samuel 16:11-12). David's righteous heart attitude didn't immediately change the situation. Shimei went along the hillside opposite David and continued cursing him, and even threw stones at him and kicked up dust. But David stood strong.

Perhaps David was inspired by Deuteronomy 23:5, when God turned Balaam's curse into a blessing because of His love for the Israelites. The Israelites didn't deserve the curse of Balaam, and the curse causeless does not land (see Proverbs 26:2). Balaam knew this, saying, "How shall I curse whom God has not cursed? And how shall I denounce whom the Lord has not denounced?" (Numbers 23:8)

In Nehemiah 13:2, we read this pivotal word about the situation: "Our God, however, turned the curse into a blessing." The wicked king exclaimed: "What have you done to me? I brought you here to curse my enemies, and behold, you have only blessed them!"

That's the power of God in action! When you discern a curse on someone's life, whether it's a financial curse, a health curse, a relational curse, or so on, ask God what blessing He wants to bring to defy the blessing—then break the curse and prophesy it.

PROPHESY

Take a moment to reflect on areas in your life, or someone else's life, where a curse has been at work—

whether it's generational, a word spoken, or a situation that has caused long-lasting negative effects. Ask the Holy Spirit to reveal any curse hindering progress, peace, or breakthrough.

Once you have clarity, begin to prophesy the blessing from the curse. God may lead you to prophesy that the curse is broken in the name of Jesus and that God's favor is now being released. He may lead you to prophesy that what was meant for harm will be turned into good and that the blessing of God will restore what was lost.

God may lead you to speak life and favor into the areas under the weight of the curse. He may inspire you to prophesy breakthrough, restoration, and divine turnaround, knowing that God's blessing is far greater than any curse spoken or inherited. Trust that as you speak, God is transforming the situation and releasing His divine favor.

ACTIVATION 77
Share What God Wants to Impart

Impartation is both a Scriptural concept and a spiritual reality. Impartation is a divine transfer that releases an ability you didn't have before. Through impartation, the Holy Spirit gives or grants you a spiritual gift, revelation, or power that you need to fulfill your purpose.

Impart means "give." It means to grant as from a store. God has a great storehouse of gifts and blessings, and He wants to impart what will strengthen someone in their calling. *Young's Literal Bible* translates this "to give a share of." Impartation is a transfer of grace from God.

In Scripture, we see an impartation of blessings from Jacob to his sons (see Genesis 28:1-4). We see the impartation of the Holy Spirit by the laying on of hands in Acts 8:14-17. We see the impartation of healing when the woman with an issue of blood for twelve years touched the hem of Jesus' garments (see Matthew 9:20-22).

Paul imparted spiritual gifts. In Romans 1:11-12, he wrote, "For I am yearning to see you, that I may impart and share with you some spiritual gift to strengthen and establish you. That is, that we may be mutually strengthened and encouraged and comforted by each other's faith, both yours and mine."

We also see an impartation for service. Remember in Acts 6 when the church was growing so fast and there was not enough help? The Hellenist widows were complaining, so the apostles chose seven men to take up the food service.

You can also receive impartation through prophecy. Moses imparted the spirit of prophecy to the 70 in Numbers 11:24-25:

"So Moses went out and told the people the words of the Lord, and he gathered the seventy men of the elders of the people and placed them around the tabernacle. Then the Lord came down in the cloud, and spoke to him, and took of the Spirit that was upon him, and placed the same upon the seventy elders; and it happened, when the Spirit rested upon them, that they prophesied, although they never did so again."

PROPHESY

Take a moment to ask the Holy Spirit to show you what God wants to impart to a specific person or group. It could be wisdom, strength, peace, or a spiritual gift. Tune your spiritual ears to hear God's heart for them, and ask Him to reveal the specific impartation they need in this season. Once you sense what God wants to release, begin to prophesy it over them and release it by faith.

ACTIVATION 78
Prophesy the Next Season

People must know what season they are in—or what season they are coming out of and what season they are about to enter into. Spiritually speaking, a season is a period of time—that can be specific or indefinite time. Not everyone has an understanding of their season.

Ecclesiastes 3:1 tells us, "To everything there is a season, and a time for every purpose under heaven." And Galatians 6:9 tells us, "Don't grow weary in well-doing because we'll reap if we don't give up—in due season."

Of course, people can be in more than one season at a time. I've been in a season of promotion, a season of consecration, and a season of intense spiritual warfare simultaneously. Even still, people need to discern the spiritual season to respond appropriately.

For example, if someone is waging warfare in a time of peace, they could stir up devils for no reason. If someone is silent when it's time to speak, they can miss an opportunity. If someone adds to their calendar when they should be cutting back, they could wind up in stressful situations.

God knows everyone's times and seasons because He is the God of our times and seasons. Daniel 2:21 plainly says, "God changes the times and seasons." David understood that our times were in His hands (see Psalm 31:15).

God always has a plan for someone. He can open doors no man can close and close doors no man can open (see Revelation 3:7-8). God can bestow crazy favor on someone and even cause their enemies to be at peace with them (Psalm 16:7).

PROPHESY

Ask the Holy Spirit to reveal the next season for someone's life. For example, it could be a transition, a shift in their assignment, or a new chapter in their spiritual walk. Ask God to give you insight into what He is about to do in their life and how He is preparing them for what's next.

Once you sense what God is showing you, begin to prophesy over them. You may, for example, prophesy how they stepping into a new season filled with God's favor, provision, and realized purpose. God may lead you to speak to the areas of growth, breakthrough, and divine opportunities that will mark their next season. He may lead you to prophesy that they are fully equipped to embrace the new opportunities God is about to bring forth, and that every transition will be smooth as they walk in alignment with His will.

ACTIVATION 79
Release a Warning

God gives prophetic warnings to and through His people throughout Scripture. The prophetic warning ministry is not relegated to prophets and watchmen only. Every believer has the ability to stand, watch, warn, and pray.

Warn means "to give notice to beforehand, especially of danger or evil; to give admonishing advice to counsel; to call to one's attention: inform," according to *Merriam-Webster*'s dictionary.

Warning is alerting someone to what is going on in the spirit realm that could cause them harm. Warning is cautioning someone about danger that lies ahead. Warning is notifying someone about what the devil is planning. Warning is preparing people for coming changes. Warning is summoning people to action.

Warning is urging people to make a move. Warning people is giving them strong advice. Warning is reproving people of behavior that will open them up to problems. Warning is directing people to a path of safety. Warning is reminding people of something they knew but forgot. Warning people is prompting them to do something. Warning people is advocating for the Lord's plan.

Can you see it? The warning ministry is multi-faceted and critical to the church. When God told Ezekiel to give the people warning for Him in Ezekiel 3:17, the Hebrew word for warning in that verse is *zahar*. According to *The KVJ Old Testament Hebrew Lexicon*, it means "to admonish, warn, teach, shine, send out light, be light, be shining."

When Jesus walked the earth, fully God and fully man, He offered many warnings. Jesus warned us about sin, hypocritical religious leaders, false prophets, false christs, the devil, hell, being judgmental, and the destruction of Jerusalem.

PROPHESY

Ask the Holy Spirit to show you someone—or a city or nation—for whom He has a warning or word of caution. Sometimes, God warns us not out of judgment but out of His love and desire to protect people. Think of a warning as a divine grace to help someone avoid harm and walk in God's best for their life.

As you focus on the person or situation, ask God for clarity. What danger or pitfall are about to walk into? Where does God want them to take heed and make adjustments before it's too late? Listen for the Holy Spirit's guidance, knowing He will reveal what is necessary for their protection and restoration.

Once you sense the Lord's heart, begin to prophesy the warning with boldness and in love. Speak with compassion and redemption—not anger or wrath— understanding that this word is meant to protect and keep them on the right path.

He may lead you to explain that this warning is a moment for redirection, not condemnation. It's a call to greater alignment with God's will and protection in His perfect purpose for their life.

ACTIVATION 80
Prophesy the Open Door

God is a door-opening God. He has all the keys to every door we need to enter to walk into our high calling and destiny. Revelation 3:8, "I know your works. See, I have set before you an open door, and no one can shut it; for you have a little strength, have kept My word, and have not denied My name."

Many people try to open doors in their own strength, but one prophetic word can clarify the doors God wants to open at any given time or season. A door, prophetically speaking, is a means of access or participation. It is a portal or gateway into something new or different.

Paul spoke about a door of faith. God can, for example, use someone to open the door of faith to a people group through evangelism. Acts 14:27 reads, "Now when they had come and gathered the church together, they reported all that God had done with them, and that He had opened the door of faith to the Gentiles."

Hosea 2:15 prophesies a door of hope: "I will give her her vineyards from there, and the Valley of Achor as a door of hope; She shall sing there, as in the days of her youth, as in the day when she came up from the land of Egypt." Paul the apostle spoke of a wide door of opportunity for his ministry in 1 Corinthian 16:9.

God is a doorkeeper and can open many different types of doors. He can open doors of increase, doors of favor, or doors of reconciliation. God can open doors of healing, wisdom, and miracles. God can open doors of relationships—even divine connections. God can open doors in ministry, like Paul, or doors in your career.

PROPHESY

Ask the Holy Spirit to show you a door that God wants to open for someone. Allow God to guide you in identifying the specific door He is opening.

As you focus on the person or situation, ask God for clarity. What is He preparing them for? What opportunity will unfold that will align with His perfect will for their life? Trust that the Holy Spirit will give you insight into the nature of this door—whether it's a door to promotion, healing, reconciliation, or a new season.

Once you receive this understanding, begin to prophesy with confidence. Prophesy life into the opportunity. Pray that every hindrance, every blockade, every door of delay is being removed, and that God's perfect timing will release this new opportunity.

Remember, you don't need the full picture to prophesy. Launch out with what you have and God is likely to fill your mouth with more.

ACTIVATION 81
Prophesy the Closed Door

Sometimes, before we can go through the open door God has ordained for our lives, another door must close. Other time, a door must close because it's giving the enemy access.

Revelation 3:8 tells us, "I know your works. See, I have set before you an open door, and no one can shut it; for you have a little strength, have kept My word, and have not denied My name."

The challenge for many people is they don't know what door to close—and they often close the wrong door and cause themselves and others trouble or pain. Other people can't discern God is closing a door, and they resist His hand or start waging war on what they think is a demonic attack. In doing so, they are only causing themselves stress and delaying their blessing.

Consider Paul the apostle's words in Philippians 3:13-14: "Brothers, I do not count myself to have attained, but this one thing I do, forgetting those things which are behind and reaching forward to those things which are ahead, I press toward the goal to the prize of the high calling of God in Christ Jesus."

It's been said that when God closes a door, He opens three more. Yet many people are in denial about closed doors in careers, relationships, ministry, and beyond. At times, a prophetic word is needed to confirm a closed door, announce a closed door, or cut through the doubt about what door God is closing so they can agree with the Lord's will.

PROPHESY

Ask the Holy Spirit to reveal to you a door that God wants to close in someone's life. As you wait on the Lord, listen for the specific area where God wants to shut the door.

Is it an open door to the enemy? Is it a door that leads them away from God's will? Allow the Holy Spirit to show you the significance of this closed door and how it will protect them from further harm or delay or make way for the new thing He wants to do.

CHAPTER 5

Advanced Prophetic Activations

When you step into advanced prophetic activations, you are moving in deeper waters, where the prophetic mantle begins to carry weightier responsibility. These exercises take you beyond the foundational principles of edification, exhortation, and comfort into dimensions where the fivefold prophet operates. This level is not for the faint of heart—it requires maturity, humility, and a willingness to yield to the Spirit of God fully.

Advanced prophetic activations challenge you to press into realms of greater accuracy and clarity, where prophetic words carry strategic insight, correction, and direction that can shift atmospheres, heal nations, and pierce through spiritual darkness.

This is where the prophet begins to function as a voice not only to individuals but also to churches, regions, and even nations. At this level, you must learn to navigate the delicate balance between delivering bold words with authority and tempering them with the love and wisdom of the Holy Spirit.

These activations will stretch you in ways that require you to depend on God like never before. You may find yourself delivering words of warning or judgment, discerning the heart of God in complex situations, or engaging in prophetic intercession that demands persistence. You need to learn how to announce and interpret times, seasons, and spiritual climates while ensuring that your words align with the written Word of God.

Stepping into this level of the prophetic requires deep consecration. You cannot accurately carry the weight of a fivefold mantle without a lifestyle of prayer, fasting, and intimacy with the Lord. And you can't make yourself a prophet. God has to call you. Jesus gave prophets (see Ephesians 4:11).

Your character must be refined, your motives pure, and your ears attuned to the whispers of the Holy Spirit. Advanced activations are not about performance—they're about obedience to the Spirit of God and surrendering your voice to be used as His instrument.

It's also vital to recognize that with greater prophetic responsibility comes greater spiritual warfare. High level prophetic ministry often takes you into confrontational realms, where the enemy seeks to silence your voice or distort your message. This is why you must be diligent in putting on the whole armor of God and walking in submission to spiritual authority. Accountability is crucial at this stage, as the words you release can carry tremendous influence and impact.

These advanced activations are designed to prepare you to function at high levels of prophetic ministry. Whether you are called to operate in a local church, a prophetic company, or to speak to nations, the exercises in this section will help you steward the prophetic gift with excellence, precision, and integrity.

Remember, God's goal is not just to use you but to transform you. As you engage in these advanced activations, allow Him to shape you into a vessel of honor, ready for every good work. It's not just about prophesying—it's about becoming the prophet He has called you to be.

Let's press into the deep together. This is where the mature prophets rise.

ACTIVATION 82
Prophesy About a Secular Singer

Secular singers need Jesus. Think about it: They carry a God-given gift to write and sing songs that glorify Jesus. But instead, many are unwittingly glorifying the enemy of their soul with perverse lyrics and lifestyles.

While some young Christian psalmists wound up going the way of the world and allowing the enemy to defile their gift, many in the secular music industry have never met the Lord.

Indeed, many gifted young hopefuls have been lured into an antichrist system that rejects—and even mocks—the King of kings and Lord of lords. Still, there is some light in Hollywood, and we have seen celebrities come to Jesus. Coming from the right heart, prophecy can be an evangelism tool in the music industry.

Remember, there's nothing wrong with fame in and of itself as long as the famous ones point back to God and His Christ. Samuel had fame. Everyone knew he was a prophet and none of his words fell to the ground. Joshua's fame was in all the land (see Joshua 6:27). Solomon was famous and the Queen of Sheba set out to meet him for herself (see 1 Kings 10:1).

Fame is not the issue. It's often the results of fame that keep a person from pursuing Christ or cause them to walk away from Him for the pleasures of this age.

PROPHESY

Ask the Holy Spirit to show you a secular musician or singer—or a backslidden Christian artist—over whom He wants you to declare His prophetic words. Start praying for that musician/singer and ask the Holy Spirit to let you see what He sees and feel what He feels about them. Out of this place of love and compassion, begin to prophesy over them.

Don't focus on judgment. God may show you their sin so you can pray, but don't issue a prophetic judgment. Focus on grace. Unless these God-gifted artists turn to the Lord, we already know heaven will not be their final destination. Without a "come to Jesus" moment where they receive Him as Lord and Savior, their eternity is horrifying.

Spend a moment listening for God's perspective on their life, their gift, and their influence. Ask Him to show you how He desires to use their voice for His purposes. Then, as God opens the opportunity, prophesy with boldness and love. Speak words of destiny, hope, and alignment with God's plan for their life, calling forth the redemptive purpose of their gift. Declare that their voice will be used for God's glory and to release His truth in the earth! It doesn't matter if they never hear the words. God's words don't return void.

ACTIVATION 83
Prophesy Into the Technology Sector

The technology sector is buzzing with heavy emphasis on cryptocurrency, the metaverse, artificial intelligence, augmented reality, virtual reality, and NFTs. Technology is certainly seeing a revolution. Then there's robotics and Web 3.

But technology is not all computerized bells and whistles. The definition of technology is "the practical application of knowledge, especially in a particular area," according to *Merriam-Webster*'s dictionary. Although crude by today's standards, Tubal-Cain used technology to make things out of bronze and iron (see Genesis 4:22). Noah used engineering technology to build an ark (see Genesis 6).

We are in a technology age that's seeing creative ministers find ways to preach the Gospel on worldly social media platforms. At the same time, technology has redefined the workplace. Changes in business travel have forced innovation beyond Zoom, including inviting speakers who appear in holograph form.

With all this, there are cyber threats. An attack by criminals can take down banking systems, electric grids and more. The bottom line is technology will be woven more and more into our daily lives, at home and at work. New technologies and technology companies are rising in the nations.

But there are also spiritual technologies. God spoke to me some years ago about new spiritual warfare technologies. There are deliverance technologies and prophetic technologies that are helping to push back darkness.

I once prophesied, "Many of us have become accustomed to waging spiritual warfare in a certain way and have seen strong results, but in this new season we may need to seek new spiritual warfare technologies— new practical applications of knowledge and an awareness of the breadth of the weapons we actually possess. Then we will have the 'capability given by the practical application of knowledge.'"

PROPHESY

What is God saying to you about the technology sector? Or, what is God saying about His technologies in the church? Ask the Holy Spirit for revelation about spiritual technologies and natural technologies. You may or may not prophesy this over a person, but you can prophesy it into the airwaves.

Ask the Holy Spirit to reveal what God is saying about the technology sector, whether it's natural or spiritual technologies. Seek insight into how God is moving within the tech industry and how His Kingdom is intersecting with the advancements of technology.

You may be led to prophesy this over a specific person or organization in the sector, or you may prophesy it into the airwaves, declaring that God is using technology to accelerate His purposes on earth, bring innovation to the church, and release tools that further His Kingdom. Speak life over these areas, calling forth divine strategies, wisdom, and breakthroughs in both natural and spiritual technologies!

ACTIVATION 84
Prophesy Over a Politician

While we don't see "politicians" in the Bible like we know them in modern times, there were ruling authorities in cities and nations, including kings and governors, magistrates, prime ministers, and other high-level advisors.

Paul the apostle put it plainly, "Let every soul be subject to the governing authorities. For there is no authority except from God, and the authorities that exist are appointed by God" (see Romans 13:1). While we are called to submit to authority, we can also prophesy over authority.

Samuel prophesied over Eli, Saul, and David. Elijah and Micaiah both prophesied over the wicked king Ahab. Elisha prophesied over Ahab's son Jehoram, as well as King Jehoshaphat. Daniel prophesied over four kings during his lifetime, serving as a voice of reason in their Babylonian territories and often finding favor.

Today, we still see prophets prophesying over politicians though most of them do it from a distance. While some prophets have access to kings, presidents, prime ministers, and governors—and are welcome to share what the Lord is saying—it's not as common in our day to have access to the highest officials in a nation.

However, that doesn't mean you can't prophesy over a politician. I prophesied over a governor in his mansion once directly. I've prophesied over mayors in their offices. But I also prophesied to Queen Elizabeth through one of her secretaries. Even if you don't have any way to get the message to the politician, there's something about prophesying it into the atmosphere.

Remember, the politician never has to hear the prophetic word for it to bear fruit. Prophetic intercessors can take the true prophetic word and wage war with it, decree it, and bathe it in prayer, and God can work behind the scenes to set the stage for its fulfillment.

PROPHESY

Look at the news and see if a particular story about a politician catches your attention. Begin to pray for them, asking the Lord to reveal His heart for their life, their decisions, and their leadership. Listen for any specific words, encouragement, or warnings that the Lord may want to release over them. Prophesy into the situation, declaring God's will for the nation, the leader, and their influence.

Alternatively, if you have a prayer burden for a specific politician, press into prayer and allow the Holy Spirit to guide you in prophesying over them into the atmosphere.

ACTIVATION 85
Prophesy Over a National Economy

Prophesying over the economy can be a challenge. Many prophetic voices decry coin shortages, hyperinflation, and absolute economic collapses without any semblance of hope. Others prophesy nothing but prosperity no matter the natural circumstances that defy their words even as they speak them.

When we prophesy into economies, we need to hear clearly what the enemy may be planning and what God wants to do and gain prophetic insight into how we should respond according to the will of God.

Zechariah 10:1 says to ask the Lord for rain in the time of rain. But Elijah asked for rain in the time of famine. Which is the right thing to do? You must press in to hear what's on God's heart, His plans, and purposes for any given city or people group. You also need to seek His timing and His strategy.

Of course, that's not to say God can't speak prophetically through you without you knowing anything at all about a nation's economy. Sometimes, that leads to the purest prophecy. However, wisdom dictates not prophesying over serious issues like national economies without knowing you have the mind of Christ on the matter.

Joseph prophesied about a famine in Egypt and received a strategy that led to the salvation of many. Elisha warned the Shunamite woman of a coming famine so she could escape to the land of the Philistines and survive. Elijah prophesied a strategy over a woman and her jar of flour and jug of oil didn't run dry during a time of drought.

Economies ebb and flow. There are boom times and bust times. Bull markets and bear markets. It's part of economic cycles.

PROPHESY

Ask God to reveal insights about the economic cycle of your nation or another nation. Seek His heart for the current state of the economy and what He desires to do in this season. Listen for any prophetic direction or strategy He wants to release into the economic system, whether it's a word of breakthrough, provision, or wisdom for financial stability—or a warning.

Don't stop at just a predictive word; if God gives you a strategy, speak it forth. Prophetically expose any enemy agendas and release divine strategies that will align the nation's financial systems with His will. God may lead you to release His wisdom for key decision-makers or declare shifts that open doors for breakthrough and long-term stability.

ACTIVATION 86
Prophesy With a Time Frame

There are times when the Holy Spirit will lead you to prophesy with a time frame attached. In other words, you prophesy that something will happen in 30 days or three years, etc. We see this in Scripture.

Elisha prophesied to the woman who was barren, "About this time next year you shall embrace a son" (2 Kings 4:16). Elisha prophesied with a time frame again during a time of great famine. In 2 Kings 7:1, he said, "Hear the word of the Lord. Thus says the Lord: 'Tomorrow about this time a seah of fine flour shall be sold for a shekel, and two seahs of barley for a shekel, at the gate of Samaria.'"

Both times, of course, Elisha was correct. Although we see too many prophetic people putting timelines on prophecies where the Lord did not give a timeline, we should not be timid about releasing the time frame of a manifestation of the prophetic word of God plainly tells us. We just have to make sure it's God really telling us.

We know this is one way God speaks because He told Pharaoh, "Behold, tomorrow about this time I will cause very heavy hail to rain down, such as has not been in Egypt since its founding until now" (Exodus 9:18). Samuel prophesied a timeline (see 1 Samuel 9:16). Jezebel made a prophetic threat with a timeline (1 Kings 19:2). Prophesying the timeline can give someone hope and urgency to obey God.

PROPHESY

Ask the Holy Spirit to reveal a specific situation or promise with a prophetic time frame. Seek God for clarity on the timing of His promises. I need to stress this: It's important to not only prophesy the word but also ask for His guidance in understanding the appointed time. God doesn't always give you the timeframe.

Once you receive the direction from the Holy Spirit, prophesy the word with faith and include the time frame God reveals (if He reveals one). For example, if you sense God is about to bring a breakthrough, He may lead you to prophesy that it will happen "within the next few months" or "before the end of this season." If there's a word of restoration, He may lead you to prophesy that it will happen "in this next year" or "in the coming weeks." Again, you must hear the timeline to prophesy it accurately. There's no ambiguity or guessing games here. Our times are in His hands (see Psalm 31:15).

He may be led to declare that His promises are not delayed but are coming to pass in His perfect timing. Prophesy with confidence, knowing that God's timing is indeed perfect, and the word He gives will not return void. As you prophesy with a time frame, encourage the person to hold onto the word, trusting that God's plan and timing will be fulfilled.

ACTIVATION 87
Prophesy Over a City

Throughout the Old and New Testaments, we see prophets prophesying over cities. God has something to say about cities, including your city.

Many prophecies in Scripture are negative, such as the destruction of Tyre in Ezekiel 26:3-14. Let's look at verses three through six so you get an idea:

"Therefore thus says the Lord God: 'Behold, I am against you, O Tyre, and will cause many nations to come up against you, as the sea causes its waves to come up. And they shall destroy the walls of Tyre and break down her towers; I will also scrape her dust from her, and make her like the top of a rock. It shall be a place for spreading nets in the midst of the sea, for I have spoken,' says the Lord God; 'it shall become plunder for the nations.

"Also her daughter villages which are in the fields shall be slain by the sword. Then they shall know that I am the Lord'."

Isaiah and Jeremiah prophesied about the destruction of Babylon. Jeremiah prophesied about the destruction of Edom. But there are also positive prophecies over cities in Scripture.

There are prophecies of restoration, for example, and Jerusalem is a prominent city in end times prophecies. Daniel, Jesus and Paul each prophesied a Jewish temple will be rebuilt in Jerusalem.

PROPHESY

Ask the Holy Spirit to open your eyes to see what God is doing in your city. Take a moment to pray and ask God for His heart for the people, the leaders, and the areas within your city.

As you wait, listen for the areas that God wants to touch—whether it's specific neighborhoods, institutions, or societal issues that need His intervention.

Once you receive a sense of direction, prophesy over your city—or the city God gave you a word about. God may lead you to prophesy His will over your city's economy, its government, its schools, or its people.

Continue to practice this exercise as frequently as you can. You can even keep track of the news in your city and wait on the Lord to tell you His thoughts, plans and purposes. Check out my prophetic and prayer courses, Prophets on the 7 Mountains and Praying the News at www.schoolofthespirit.tv

In this way, you will learn to speak as a prophetic voice in your city, releasing words God's divine purposes. Prophesy with faith, knowing that God desires to bless and redeem every part of your city.

ACTIVATION 88
Prophesy Over a Celebrity

Some people get prophetic words for celebrities. I've known many people who have experienced this. Usually, people have no access to these celebrities, but that doesn't mean you can't still prophesy the word.

Yes, it's ideal for someone to hear the prophetic word over their life and agree with it, yield to it, and war with it until it comes to pass. But such access to celebrities is not always possible. Sometimes, then, you have to prophesy a thing into the atmosphere and take a stand for that prophecy in intercession. You have to pray that God would work in them (or work out of them) what needs to change to align with His will as revealed in the prophetic word He gave you.

Isaiah 55:11 says clearly, "So shall My word be that goes forth from My mouth; It shall not return to Me void, But it shall accomplish what I please, And it shall prosper in the thing for which I sent it."

While most personal prophecy is conditional, if God spoke to you about a celebrity, He spoke for a reason. God is a God of purpose. He's not random. So go ahead and prophesy the word as if the person was standing right there in front of you. And then pray it through as a burden of the Lord for the soul of the one who may not know Him.

PROPHESY

Ask the Holy Spirit to highlight a celebrity—someone in the public eye who may need a word of encouragement, direction, or breakthrough. This could be someone you've seen in the media, in movies, in sports, or any famous person the Lord brings to your heart. Take a moment to pray for them, asking God for any prophetic insight He wants to release.

As you wait on the Lord, listen carefully for what He wants to say. Ask God to give you wisdom and discernment in delivering the word, knowing His heart is to see them walk in His purpose. God may lead you to speak life over their career, relationships, and personal struggles. He may lead you to declare that they will know God's will, or that He will use their platform for His glory.

Even if you are not speaking to them directly, prophesy into the atmosphere over their life, trusting that God can work through your words to bring about change. Trust that the prophetic word you release will plant seeds of transformation, even in the most unlikely places.

ACTIVATION 89
Prophesy Over a Prophet

Prophesying over another prophet is intimidating for some people, but if you have the word of the Lord in your mouth, it can be a blessing for you and the prophet. Think about it. Prophets pour and pour and pour some more. But who is ministering to the prophets?

When I gather with Cindy Jacobs and other prophets at our annual Apostolic Council of Prophetic Elders meeting in Dallas, there is a lot of prophecy going forth over prophets. It's not just a time to collectively seek the Lord for His Word for the Body of Christ; it's also a time when many prophets get refreshed or receive new direction.

In Scripture, we see David—who Scripture calls a prophet—surrounded by prophets and seers. There was first Samuel, then Nathan, and later Gad. Samuel prophesied David's kingship when he was still a ruddy boy. Nathan is perhaps best remembered for rebuking David, but he also had a strong word for him in 2 Samuel 7:12-16:

"When your days are fulfilled and you rest with your fathers, I will set up your seed after you, who will come from your body, and I will establish his kingdom. He shall build a house for My name, and I will establish the throne of his kingdom forever. I will be his Father, and he shall be My son.

"If he commits iniquity, I will chasten him with the rod of men and with the blows of the sons of men. But My mercy shall not depart from him, as I took it from Saul, whom I removed from before you. And your house and your kingdom shall be established forever before you. Your throne shall be established forever'."

David received the prophetic encouragement and went right to the Lord in thanks and praise. Prophets need prophetic ministry, too.

PROPHESY

Ask the Holy Spirit to bring to mind a prophet—whether someone you know personally or a public figure in the prophetic ministry. Take a moment to pray for them, asking God to reveal His heart for this person and any areas where they need encouragement, direction, wisdom, or strength. A prophet's journey can be full of challenges, so seek God's insight into what He wants to speak to them in this season.

As you begin to pray, listen for the Holy Spirit's guidance on what to declare. He may lead you to prophesy words of strength, endurance, and clarity. He may lead you to speak life into their prophetic calling, declaring that God will continue to sharpen their discernment, give them fresh revelation, and protect their hearts from weariness. He may lead you to declare that they will continue to stand firm in their calling, even in the face of opposition, and that God will give them a deeper understanding of His plans.

Trust that your words will strengthen and refuel them, empowering them to continue in the high calling of the prophetic.

ACTIVATION 90
Prophesy Repentance

Part and parcel of the prophet's mandate is to call forth repentance. This is not a popular task. Indeed, this is part of what makes prophets an enemy to the world—and to the lukewarm or rebellious in the church.

Nevertheless, throughout the pages of the Bible, we see prophets calling people and nations to repentance. This was not a carnal call based on the prophet's personal displeasure alone. It was a Holy Spirit-inspired call to bring conviction that leads to a contrite heart and restoration to God's perfect will. Let me share just one example, though there are many:

"O Israel, return to the Lord your God, for you have stumbled because of your iniquity; Take words with you, and return to the Lord. Say to Him, 'Take away all iniquity; Receive us graciously, for we will offer the sacrifices of our lips. Assyria shall not save us, we will not ride on horses, nor will we say anymore to the work of our hands, You are our gods. For in You the fatherless finds mercy" (Hosea 14:1-3).

Remember, when we prophesy repentance—make a call to repentance as inspired by the Holy Spirit—we must ensure we don't have common ground with the sin we're calling out. Put another way, we need to repent before we call others to repentance.

It's never comfortable to call for repentance, but remember that it's part and parcel of the prophetic ministry. Jesus called for repentance. In Matthew 4:17, we read, "From that time Jesus began to preach and to say, 'Repent, for the kingdom of heaven is at hand.'"

Pray and ask the Lord for a clear call to repentance. Perhaps the call is over a city or a company or some other corporate group.

PROPHESY

Ask the Holy Spirit to reveal areas where repentance is needed—either in your own life or those around you. Repentance is a powerful key that opens the door to restoration, breakthrough, and healing. Ask God to show you the specific areas where repentance will bring transformation, alignment, and greater intimacy with Him.

Once the Holy Spirit shows you these areas, begin to prophesy repentance. This must be done with grace and the heart of the Father. You are not the judge and Jesus is not condemning His people (see Romans 8:1). If you are prophesying to an individual, do this privately, like Nathan did with David.

If this is a corporate call to repentance, God may lead you to call forth a spirit of repentance, urging individuals to align their hearts with His will, turn away from sin, and return to His loving embrace. God may also lead you to prophesy the aftermath of repentance, such as the restoration or healing of the land. Be willing and obedient.

ACTIVATION 91
The Unlikely Prophet

You may see yourself as an unlikely prophet, but don't let anyone judge the gift God put in you. Amos was a farmer, and it seems he struggled with his identity as a prophet even after God started using him. In Amos 7:10-15 (NLT), we see the struggle and how his internal struggle attracted rejection in his ministry:

"Then Amaziah, the priest of Bethel, sent a message to Jeroboam, king of Israel: 'Amos is hatching a plot against you right here on your very doorstep! What he is saying is intolerable. He is saying, 'Jeroboam will soon be killed, and the people of Israel will be sent away into exile.'"

"Then Amaziah sent orders to Amos: 'Get out of here, you prophet! Go on back to the land of Judah, and earn your living by prophesying there! Don't bother us with your prophecies here in Bethel. This is the king's sanctuary and the national place of worship!'"

"But Amos replied, 'I'm not a professional prophet, and I was never trained to be one. I'm just a shepherd, and I take care of sycamore-fig trees. But the Lord called me away from my flock and told me, 'Go and prophesy to my people in Israel.'"

With that, Amos prophesied. Notice how Amos didn't see himself as a prophet. Other translations, "I am not a prophet, nor am I the son of a prophet." He didn't feel comfortable stepping into his God-given identity as a prophet nor did people didn't take him seriously. You don't have to flaunt that you are a prophet, but you should see yourself walking in the high calling God has given you.

REFLECT

Take a moment and reflect. If you struggle with standing in the office of a prophet or releasing the prophetic word that God has entrusted to you, ask yourself why. Ask the Holy Spirit why—and listen.

It's common to feel inadequate or unworthy to stand as a mouthpiece for God, but you must understand that God often calls the unlikely. If God has anointed you to be a prophet, then He has equipped you, no matter what your past looks like or how unqualified you feel.

Allow the Holy Spirit to bring to light the areas in your life where fear, insecurity, or even the sting of past rejection might be holding you back. Is it fear of what others will think? Is it imposter syndrome? Do not let those fears keep you from stepping into your full calling. God chooses the unlikely, the ones who may seem overlooked or unqualified, and He empowers them for the task at hand.

Take a step of courage and confront those fears. Repent for any agreement you've made with lies about your calling. Renounce those feelings of inadequacy and insecurity. You are called, chosen, and equipped by the Holy Spirit. Declare over yourself that you are no longer bound by fear or doubt, but you walk in the boldness and authority of the prophetic voice of God.

If you have confirmation that God has called you as a five-fold prophet (and this is not true for everyone reading this book) confess over yourself right now: I am God's prophet. I carry His word, and I will speak with boldness and clarity. No longer will I shrink back in fear or hesitation. The Spirit of the Lord is upon me, and I will release the prophetic word with confidence.

Trust that as you rise up in faith, the Lord will give you the courage and the strength to fulfill your calling. The enemy's lies will not hold you back anymore. You are His vessel, His messenger, and you will speak forth His truth! Check out my courses, Developing Prophetic Boldness and Building Prophetic Confidence, as well as other prophetic training at www.schoolofthespirit.tv.

ACTIVATION 92
Prophesy a Command

You've heard of directive words, but have you heard of commanding words? Haggai released a strong command to Israel to rebuild the temple. Let's take a literal look in Haggai 1:1-14:

"In the second year of King Darius, in the sixth month, on the first day of the month, the word of the Lord came by Haggai the prophet to Zerubbabel the son of Shealtiel, governor of Judah, and to Joshua the son of Jehozadak, the high priest, saying, 'Thus speaks the Lord of hosts, saying: 'This people says, 'The time has not come, the time that the Lord's house should be built.'

"Then the word of the Lord came by Haggai the prophet, saying, 'Is it time for you yourselves to dwell in your paneled houses, and this temple to lie in ruins?' Now therefore, thus says the Lord of hosts: 'Consider your ways! You have sown much, and bring in little; You eat, but do not have enough; You drink, but you are not filled with drink; You clothe yourselves, but no one is warm;

And he who earns wages, earns wages to put into a bag with holes.'

"Thus says the Lord of hosts: 'Consider your ways! Go up to the mountains and bring wood and build the temple, that I may take pleasure in it and be glorified,' says the Lord. 'You looked for much, but indeed it came to little; and when you brought it home, I blew it away. Why?' says the Lord of hosts. 'Because of My house that is in ruins, while every one of you runs to his own house.:

This is a high level prophetic utterance and should not be released without the leading of divine authority. People often supersede their authority in the prophetic and their words are rejected. Remember the timing, context and delivery method before releasing a prophetic command. Check out my course on prophetic authority and rankings at *www.schoolofthespirit.tv*.

PROPHESY

Quiet your spirit and tune your heart to the Lord. As His prophets, we are not just releasing random words—we are speaking His command. The Lord does not give His word without purpose. When He speaks, He gives us commands that align with His will, Kingdom, and purposes on earth.

Ask the Holy Spirit to reveal to you His heart for this moment. What command does He want to release through you today? It could be a decree of breakthrough or a command for healing and restoration. The key is to speak as the Lord has instructed, not as your emotions or limitations would direct.

Don't hesitate or second-guess what you hear when you know you heard rightly. The Lord's commands carry weight and power. Prophesy what you hear boldly, knowing that when you speak in His name, you activate heaven's will on earth. Whether you are speaking into a situation, a person's life, or even over a region, you are releasing the authority with God's command.

Remember, when God speaks, things change. When He commands, mountains move. Begin to prophesy the Lord's command over whatever He has shown you. Declare His will, His word, and His purposes into the atmosphere. When you speak His words, they are backed by divine authority and that heaven moves when you speak in obedience to His command.

As you prophesy, stand firm in the assurance that you are releasing God's divine authority. Speak with the confidence that only His commands bring—knowing that they are sure, unshakable, and unstoppable.

ACTIVATION 93
Asking God Questions

Prophets tend to be inquisitive. God doesn't mind when we ask Him questions in the right spirit. That's how we learn. Put another way; there's a difference between asking God a question out of curiosity, disappointment, or desperation and questioning God.

In his exasperation, the prophet Habakkuk asked the Lord (Hab. 1:2-4), "O Lord, how long shall I cry, and You will not hear? Even cry out to You, 'Violence!' and You will not save. Why do You show me iniquity, and cause me to see trouble?

"For plundering and violence are before me; There is strife, and contention arises. Therefore the law is powerless, and justice never goes forth. For the wicked surround the righteous; Therefore perverse judgment proceeds."

God answered the prophet speedily in Habakkuk 1:5-11. We'll look just at the first two verses for our purposes: "Look among the nations and watch—Be utterly astounded! For I will work a work in your days which you would not believe, though it were told you. For indeed I am raising up the Chaldeans, a bitter and hasty nation."

Notice how God gave the prophet an assignment: Get in your watchtower! Habakkuk then asked God another kind of question: "Are You not from everlasting, O Lord my God, my Holy One?" (Habakkuk 1:12). This, of course, was a rhetorical question acknowledging His power and sovereignty.

Habakkuk was satisfied with God's answer and in Habakkuk 2:1, we see his response: "I will stand my watch and set myself on the rampart, and watch to see what He will say to me, and what I will answer when I am corrected."

Don't wait for God to give you a download randomly. Ask Him questions, and stay on your post. He will answer you at the right time.

REFLECTION

In prophetic ministry, the questions we ask God can open doors to greater understanding, breakthroughs, and revelation. It's not just about what we ask, but how we ask. God delights in revealing Himself and His will, but we need to approach Him with the right heart and posture.

First, take a moment to reflect on your current circumstances. What is weighing on your heart? What do you need clarity on? Before you ask anything, make sure you are aligning your heart with God's purposes. Remember, our questions should be motivated by a desire to know His will and to receive His guidance, not to manipulate outcomes or fulfill selfish desires.

Begin by seeking God with humility, knowing that He is the source of all wisdom. Ask Him, "What is Your will in this situation? What do You want me to understand? How do You want me to respond?"

Approach Him with an open heart, ready to hear whatever He has to say. Don't be afraid to ask specific questions, but make sure they reflect your desire to grow and move in alignment with His purposes.

As you wait on the Lord, listen carefully for His response. Trust that He will speak, whether through Scripture, a still small voice, or a divine revelation. If the answer doesn't come immediately, don't be discouraged. Keep asking, seeking, and knocking (Matthew 7:7). Keep waiting. God promises that if we seek Him with all our hearts, we will find Him.

ACTIVATION 94
Prophesy to the False Prophets

False prophets are rising, just like Jesus said they would. There is a prophetic showdown, of sorts, coming like Elijah's confrontation of the prophets at Mt. Carmel. True prophets must speak out about false prophetic practices, as many believers are so hungry for a word they do not discern the true from the false.

God charged Micah with prophesying to the false prophets. Micah 3:5-6 reads: "Thus says the Lord concerning the prophets who make my people stray; Who chant 'Peace' While they chew with their teeth, but who prepare war against him who puts nothing into their mouths:

"Therefore you shall have night without vision, and you shall have darkness without divination; the sun shall go down on the prophets, and the day shall be dark for them. So the seers shall be ashamed, and the diviners abashed; Indeed they shall all cover their lips; For there is no answer from God."

When we prophesy to or about the false prophets, we are not condemning them. It is not our place to condemn. Remember, false prophets are intentionally leading people astray. A false prophet is not one who merely releases an inaccurate word. It's about the motive.

God had plenty to say to and about false prophets in Scripture. I, too, have prophesied to and about false prophets. What is God saying about false prophets? Prophesy!

PROPHESY

As a prophetic vessel, there may be times when God will call you to confront false prophets or false prophecy and expose their deception. This is not about personal judgment but about aligning with God's will to protect His people from harm and ensure that His truth is upheld.

Take a moment to examine your heart. Are you willing to stand boldly and speak against what does not align with God's truth, even if it's uncomfortable or controversial? Next, ask the Holy Spirit to reveal to you any false prophets who may be operating around you, whether in your community, ministry or even within your own life.

Ask for clarity and discernment to accurately identify the falsehoods and speak truth into the situation. Just as God gave Ezekiel the words to confront false prophets (Ezekiel 13:1-23), He will give you the authority and the words to confront error when He releases you to do it.

Pray that God will give you the courage to prophesy against the lies and deceptions spoken in His name—but, of course, only do this if He leads. He may not charge you with calling it out immediately or ever. Or He may call you to pray for them for a season. This kind of task requires great wisdom.

If He gives you the green light, prophesy in boldness, knowing that you are speaking in alignment with God's will. Speak with love, but also with authority, as the Spirit of the Lord leads you to bring correction, exposure, and ultimately, restoration where needed. Trust that God's Word will stand, and that the power of His truth will expose every counterfeit.

Declare over yourself: "I will be a mouthpiece of truth, and I will speak boldly against the lies of the enemy. I will not be intimidated, but I will stand for the Word of God, knowing that His truth will set His people free."

ACTIVATION 95
Discover Your Prophetic Burden

Habakkuk starts his book with a telling line, "The burden which the prophet Habakkuk saw" (Habakkuk 1:1).

Habakkuk saw the burden before he carried the burden. What is God speaking to you? What is your assignment? What is your burden?

First, understand what a burden is, biblically speaking. The Hebrew word for "burden" in Habakkuk 1:1 is "massa." It means load, bearing, burden, lifting, carrying, utterance, and oracle. Notice how the burden doesn't just mean a load but is connected with an utterance.

Your prophetic burden may be a people group to whom God calls you to prophesy encouragement—or judgment. Your prophetic burden may be prophesying strategies to leaders in your midst. Your prophetic burden may be prophesying to one of the seven mountains of society.

Once you discover your prophetic burden, you will be most effective in your ministry. You may prophesy in other areas, but when you carry the load God calls you to carry prophetically, you will sense His grace and ease in your vocation.

There is a danger, though, with prophetic burdens. The danger is trying to carry, lift, and bear the load in your own strength. Remember, Jesus said His yoke is easy, and His burden is light (see Matthew 11:30). You are not just burden-bearing *for* the Lord; you are burden-bearing *with* the Lord. You are co-laboring with Christ in the prophetic ministry to root out, pull down, destroy, throw down, build and plant (see Jeremiah 1:10).

REFLECT

A prophetic burden is a divine weight that God places on your heart. It's a deep, often overwhelming call to intercede, speak, and release His will over a specific situation, person, or region. It's a burden that stirs you from the inside out, compelling you to take action and step into the prophetic realm with authority.

Begin by asking the Holy Spirit to help you identify your prophetic burden. What stirs your heart? What causes you to feel deeply for someone, a situation, or even an entire nation? It may be something that God has placed within you for years, or it could be a new calling you've never fully recognized until now. Take time to listen—sometimes, the burden can feel like an emotional weight, a deep stirring that doesn't leave you.

Ask God to reveal the nature of your burden. Is it for healing, restoration, justice, or breakthrough? Does He want you to prophesy to a specific people group, a region, or political situation? Allow the Holy Spirit to guide you as He brings clarity to your assignment. Once you identify your prophetic burden, surrender it to God and ask for the grace to carry it well.

Now, prophesy in line with your prophetic burden, declaring that God's will shall be done, and that the power of the Holy Spirit will bring forth fruit from the words you speak.

ACTIVATION 96
Prophesy Correction

While the simple gift of prophecy is edification, exhortation and comfort, the office of the prophet sometimes releases correction. Haggai was charged with such a task in the first chapter of the book that bears his name. It was the second year of King Darius' reign when

Haggai prophesied to the governor of Judah and the high priest. Haggai 1:4-9:

"Is it time for you yourselves to dwell in your paneled houses, and this]temple to lie in ruins?" Now therefore, thus says the Lord of hosts: "Consider your ways! You have sown much, and bring in little; You eat, but do not have enough; You drink, but you are not filled with drink; You clothe yourselves, but no one is warm; And he who earns wages, earns wages to put into a bag with holes."

"Thus says the Lord of hosts: 'Consider your ways! Go up to the mountains and bring wood and build the temple, that I may take pleasure in it and be glorified,' says the Lord. 'You looked for much, but indeed it came to little; and when you brought it home, I blew it away. Why?' says the Lord of hosts.

"'Because of My house that is in ruins, while every one of you runs to his own house. Therefore the heavens above you withhold the dew, and the earth withholds its fruit. For I called for a drought on the land and the mountains, on the grain and the new wine and the oil, on whatever the ground brings forth, on men and livestock, and on all the labor of your hands.'"

This is a serious correction and Haggai also went on to prophesy the consequences if Israel didn't get it together. Prophesying correction should not be comfortable for you—and you should always check your own heart first to make sure you are in line with God's will.

PROPHESY

There are times when God calls us to prophesy correction. This isn't about condemnation or judgment but about loving truth and setting things back on course. When the Holy Spirit stirs your heart to speak correction, it's always with the goal of restoration and alignment with His will.

First, ask the Holy Spirit to examine your own heart. Are you approaching this moment with humility and a heart of love? Don't go any further until you settle this matter. If the Lord is calling you to release a word of correction, do so with the understanding that it's a tool for redemption and not rejection.

Ask God to show you the specific area that needs correction—whether in your own life, in a ministry, or within the Body of Christ. What needs to be realigned with God's will? What is out of order that God wants to set right? Trust that the Holy Spirit will give you insight and clarity.

When you receive this revelation, begin to prophesy with love but also with authority. Correct with kindness, as the Bible says in 2 Timothy 2:25, "gently instructing those who oppose." You have been given the authority to speak God's word, even in correction, and He will honor your obedience.

ACTIVATION 97
Prophesy God's Kairos

God is perfect, and His timing is perfect. We Christians, on the other hand, often get out of God's perfect timing. Ecclesiastes 3:1 tells us plainly, "To everything there is a season, a time for every purpose under heaven." God has an ordained a perfect time—or a kairos time—for every breakthrough in our lives. Our times are in His hands (see Psalm 31:15).

Consider the words of Job: "Since his days are determined, The number of his months is with You; You have appointed his limits, so that he cannot pass" (Job 14:5). God is not just the author and finisher of our faith, He is the author of time, and He sees the end from the beginning (see Isaiah 46:10). He already knows the timing of everything under the sun—and His timing is perfect just as He is perfect.

At times, God will give you lead you to prophetically announce a kairos time to a person or group. Make the prophetic announcement with as many details about what the kairos time involves as possible. This will build faith and urgency to cooperate with God. He can also use you to announce a kairos time is coming so they can prepare. This can encourage people who have struggled with long-term circumstances that don't seem to budge.

Ask God for a prophetic word about a kairos time for someone. But be careful not to add to or take away from such words. Don't presume or assume what the kairos season entails if you don't have specifics. Sometimes, it's enough for them to know the kairos time is here or is coming.

PROPHESY

Timing is everything in the Kingdom of God. It's not just about what God wants to do, but when He wants to do it. Quiet your spirit and ask the Holy Spirit to reveal to you God's kairos time in a situation or for a person. Are they waiting for a breakthrough? Is someone in your life struggling with impatience, wondering when God will move? Begin by asking God for insight into His perfect timing for their life or circumstance.

As you listen, ask God to show you the kairos season He has ordained for the person, ministry, or situation you are praying for. Ask Him when that season is coming. Maybe it's now! Ask Him for a word of direction related to a kairos moment. Are they in a season of preparation? If so, how should they prepare? Is it time to step into the kairos moment? What else do they need to know?

God may lead you to prophesy that it's a kairos time for open doors, for example, or that it is a kairos time of restoration, deliverance or healing.

ACTIVATION 98
Ask God for a Word Over the Nations

Jesus said in the last days nation would rise against nation. We know there are sheep nations and goat nations. For example, Psalm 33:12 says, "Blessed is the nation whose God is the Lord" and Isaiah 60:12 tells us, "The nation and kingdom that will not serve you shall perish; those nations shall be utterly laid to waste."

Jeremiah once prophesied over Israel, "O house of Israel, can I not do with you as this potter?" says the Lord. "Look, as the clay is in the potter's hand, so are you in My hand, O house of Israel! The instant I speak concerning a nation and concerning a kingdom, to pluck up, to pull down, and to destroy it, if that nation against whom I have spoken turns from its evil, I will relent of the disaster that I thought to bring upon it. And the instant I speak concerning a nation and concerning a kingdom, to build and to plant it, if it does evil in My sight so that it does not obey My voice, then I will relent concerning the good with which I said I would benefit it."

Just as people have destinies, so do nations—and we are called to make disciples of all nations. There's a remnant in every nation. In heaven, we'll see every tongue, tribe, and nation (see Revelation 7:9). God wants to give His prophets insight into nations so we can pray accurately and prepare rightly.

Consider the words of the prophet Habakkuk, "Look around [you, Habakkuk, replied the Lord] among the nations and see! And be astonished! Astounded! For I am putting into effect a work in your days [such] that you would not believe it if it were told you" (Habakkuk 1:5, AMPC).

You don't have to be a prophet to the nations, per se, for the Lord to share His warnings for a nation or His words of encouragement for a nation.

PROPHESY

Take a moment to quiet your mind and position your heart to hear from the Lord. Ask Him for a prophetic word for a nation—whether it's the nation you live in or a nation God places on your heart.

Pray and ask the Holy Spirit to reveal His heart for that nation. What is God doing in the nation right now? What are the areas of breakthrough, judgment, or blessing that He wants to highlight? Ask Him for wisdom and discernment to receive His heart for the leaders, the people, and the spiritual atmosphere of that nation.

As you seek the Lord, listen carefully for what He reveals. He may give you visions, Scriptures, or a specific word that speaks to the destiny or the current condition of the nation. Prophesy the word you hear over that nation.

If you sense God's call for repentance, speak it boldly, knowing it's for the nation's good. That said, if you receive heavy words for a nation, such as warnings or judgments, you need to submit those words to other prophets to judge. You need to pray through those words. Some have been reckless with releasing judgment and unwittingly released a curse.

ACTIVATION 99
Prophesy a Directional Word

While the simple gift of prophecy edifies, comforts, and exhorts, prophets can prophesy directional words. Put another way, prophets can prophesy a course of action. Someone may be wondering, "Where do I go from here in my career or in my life? What is the right course of action for my next season."

Directional words are higher than the simple gift, but they can bring confirmation and clarity to people seeking God's perfect will for their lives. Directional words can also be prophetic announcements. In other words, Jesus can give someone a new charge, assignment, or commission through a prophetic word.

One example in Scripture is found in the book of Acts. "As they ministered to the Lord and fasted, the Holy Spirit said, 'Now separate to Me Barnabas and Saul for the work to which I have called them.' Then, having fasted and prayed, and laid hands on them, they sent them away" (Acts 13:2-3). That was a directional word—

and it was not confirmation. It was leaning more toward a prophetic announcement.

Cindy Jacobs once prophesied over me a word about raising campus warriors. That was not a confirmation. It was a directional word that came with an assignment and a commissioning. Without prophetic direction, some may fall into the snare of going the way that seems right in their mind, which violates Scripture and can bring them to destruction.

Proverbs 3:5-6 tells us, "Trust in the Lord with all your heart, and lean not on your own understanding; In all your ways acknowledge Him, and He shall direct your paths." When someone is confused about what the next step is in their life, God can send a prophet with a directional word that paves the way for His will to be done.

During a famine, Elijah told a widow to bring him a drink of water and make a little cake for him. Her response was grim. She said she was going to eat one last meal with her son and die.

Elijah gave her a prophetic direction, "And Elijah said to her, 'Do not fear; go and do as you have said, but make me a small cake from it first, and bring it to me; and afterward make some for yourself and your son. For thus says the Lord God of Israel: 'The bin of flour shall not be used up, nor shall the jar of oil run dry, until the day the Lord sends rain on the earth.'" (1 Kings 17:13-14).

PROPHESY

Start by quieting your mind and asking the Holy Spirit to give you a clear understanding of the situation at hand. Ask God to reveal His perfect will and timing for the person or circumstance you pray for. Is there a decision that needs to be made? Is there a path that needs to be chosen? Let God speak into the situation and give you direction.

As you wait on God, listen closely. He may speak to you through Scripture, a still small voice, or an impression on your heart. When you receive the word, speak it out with authority. He may also prophesy specific steps to take. If God has shown you what action needs to be taken, release that word boldly.

ACTIVATION 100
Prophesy in Song

You don't have to be a singer to prophesy in song. One time at our Elijah Company intensive for prophets and highly prophetic people, I began to sing out about how weeping may endure for a night, but now it's morning. I kept prophesying in song, "It's morning. It's morning. It's morning." It might not have sounded like Amy Grant but my song carried an anointing that broke yokes of bondage off people.

We see the prophetic song in Scripture. We call it "the song of the Lord." I wrote more about this in my book, *The Prophet's Devotional.*

Deborah sang the song of the Lord, or what some call a victory hymn. Miriam also sang the song of the Lord after Moses led the people through the Red Sea (see Exod. 15). Later, Mary sang the song of the Lord after visiting Elizabeth and discovering she, too, was pregnant.

Luke 1:49-55 offers one example from Mary, "For the Mighty One is holy, and he has done great things for me.

He shows mercy from generation to generation to all who fear him. His mighty arm has done tremendous things! He has scattered the proud and haughty ones. He has brought down princes from their thrones and exalted the humble. He has filled the hungry with good things and sent the rich away with empty hands. He has helped his servant Israel and remembered to be merciful. For he made this promise to our ancestors, to Abraham and his children forever."

Ask God for the song of the Lord over someone's life. Don't worry if you don't sing well.

PROPHESY

Invite the Holy Spirit to give you a melody and words that carry His heart for someone. Begin to sing spontaneously, allowing the Spirit to guide your voice and lyrics as you release encouragement, hope, or breakthrough over their life. It's a good idea to record yourself, if you can, as you may forget the melody or words. Trust the flow of the Spirit as you prophesy through song, knowing that your melody carries His power to uplift, heal, and transform!

ACTIVATION 101
Prophesy the Revival God Wants to Bring

God is a God of revival. Although the word "revival" itself is not in the Bible, the concept of reviving is.

Isaiah 57:15 reads, "For this is what the high and exalted One says— he who lives forever, whose name is holy: "I live in a high and holy place, but also with the one who is contrite and lowly in spirit, to revive the spirit of the lowly and to revive the heart of the contrite."

Psalm 85:6 continues, "Will you not revive us again, that your people may rejoice in you?" Psalm 80:18 says, "Then we will not turn away from you; revive us, and we will call on your name." And Psalm 19:7 says, "The law of the Lord is perfect, reviving the soul; the testimony of the Lord is sure, making wise the simple."

What is revival? As I wrote in *The Revivalist's Devotional*, It's a renewed interest in God. It's a return to our first love. It's a restoration in our families. It's taking something dead and breathing life upon it. It's reactivating something that is not flourishing.

Hosea 6:2 says, "After two days he will revive us; on the third day he will raise us up, that we may live before him." That paints a picture of a people who are suffering and need a move of God in their life.

God not only revives churches, but He revives relationships, businesses, finances, and more. God is a God of revival.

PROPHESY

Take a moment to reflect on the areas where God wants to bring revival—whether it's in a person's life, a community, a city, or even in a particular circumstance. Ask the Holy Spirit to reveal to you where revival is needed and what it would look like. Revival can come in many forms: healing, breakthrough, awakening, restoration, or a fresh outpouring of God's Spirit.

As you receive this revelation, start to prophesy about those areas. God may guide you to declare that the wind of His Spirit will blow over specific dry places, awakening them to life. He may also inspire you to prophesy revival over dormant gifts and callings, reactivating purpose in them.

God may lead you to prophetically call forth the transformation and healing that revival brings. Prophesy His promises of restoration and breakthrough, knowing that God is always faithful to bring renewal and fresh life to His people.

CONCLUSION

You can revisit these activations time and time again, and the Holy Spirit will reveal something new with every encounter. That's the beauty of walking in the prophetic—the more you press into God's heart, the more He unveils layers of His truth, mysteries, and plans. Indeed, He rewards those who diligently seek Him (see Hebrews 11:6).

These exercises are a starting point, but they're also a launching pad for deeper exploration. Let them stir your spiritual imagination, and don't hesitate to create your own activations inspired by the principles found in this book.

Don't wait for the Lord to ask, "What do you see?" Ask Him today, "Lord, what do You see?" and trust Him to open your eyes to His perspective. Follow Jesus' encouragement in Matthew 7:7 (AMPC): "Keep on asking and it will be given you; keep on seeking and you will find; keep on knocking [reverently] and [the door] will be opened to you."

The prophetic lifestyle is one of persistence and pursuit. Your hunger for His voice will draw you closer to His heart, and as you lean in, you'll begin to see with greater clarity, hear with sharper accuracy, and speak with heaven's authority.

Much like learning to play an instrument, honing any spiritual gift takes intentionality. It's not a one-time event—it's a journey of exercising your faith, stretching your capacity, and surrendering to the Holy Spirit. This is how you sharpen your spiritual senses and cultivate a lifestyle where hearing God's voice becomes as natural as breathing. But it starts with hunger—a deep longing to see what God is showing, hear what He is saying, and respond with obedience and faith.

Let me encourage you: don't stop here. Let this book mark the beginning of a new dimension in your prophetic journey. The prophetic is not just about releasing words—it's about building intimacy with the Father, stepping into the unseen, and partnering with heaven to shift things on earth. The activations in this book are tools, but the true power lies in your willingness to step out in faith and trust God to meet you in the process.

As you move forward, I want to pray over you:

Father, in the name of Jesus, ignite a holy hunger in the hearts of Your people—a hunger to see what You see, hear what You hear, and speak what You are saying. Open their eyes to the angelic dimension, to the secret places in Your Kingdom, and even to the wicked counsel of the enemy so they can intercede and decree Your plans. Grant them visions like Ezekiel saw, understanding like Daniel carried, and boldness like Jeremiah walked in. Let their prophetic gift be sanctified for Your glory.

Teach them to set their gaze on You alone, to turn their eyes from worthless things, and to walk in purity of vision. Empower them to become Your voice in the earth, releasing life, truth, and destiny wherever they go. May they walk in step with Your Spirit, overflowing with Your love, wisdom, and authority. In Jesus' name, amen.

The prophetic journey is one of continual discovery and awe. So don't stop here. Keep asking, keep seeking, and keep knocking. The Lord is ready to take you deeper if you are willing to go. He has so much more to show you, and as you walk this path of obedience, your voice will grow sharper, your faith will grow stronger, and your life will radiate His glory.

This is your season to rise up as His voice. The world is waiting. Remember, check out School of the Spirit for more training.

—Jennifer LeClaire

ABOUT JENNIFER LECLAIRE

Jennifer LeClaire is an internationally recognized author, apostolic-prophetic voice to her generation, and conference speaker. She carries a reforming voice that inspires and challenges believers to pursue intimacy with God, cultivate their spiritual gifts and walk in the fullness of what God has called them to do.

Jennifer is contending for awakening in the nations through intercession and spiritual warfare, strong apostolic preaching and practical prophetic teaching that equips the saints for the work of the ministry.

Jennifer is senior leader of Awakening House of Prayer in Fort Lauderdale, FL, founder of the Ignite Network and founder of the Awakening Prayer Hubs prayer movement.

Jennifer formerly served as the first-ever editor of *Charisma* magazine. Jennifer is a prolific author who has written over 60 books. Some of her materials have been translated into Spanish, French, Chinese, Romanian, Dutch, and Korean.

Jennifer was ordained by Bishop Bill Hamon, founder of Christian International. She is also part of the United States Coalition of Apostolic Leaders and the International Society of Deliverance Ministers.

Jennifer has a powerful testimony of God's power to set the captives free and claim beauty for ashes. She shares her story with women who need to understand the love and grace of God in a lost and dying world. You can also learn more about Jennifer in her short film, Vindicated at jenniferleclaire.org/vindicatedfilm.

OTHER BOOKS BY JENNIFER LECLAIRE

Decoding Your Dreams
The Spiritual Warrior's Guide to Defeating Water Spirits
Releasing the Angels of Abundant Harvest
The Heart of the Prophetic
A Prophet's Heart
The Making of a Prophet
The Spiritual Warrior's Guide to Defeating Jezebel Did the Spirit of God Say That?
Satan's Deadly Trio
Jezebel's Puppets
The Spiritual Warfare Battle Plan
Waging Prophetic Warfare
Dream Wild!
Faith Magnified
Fervent Faith
Breakthrough!
Mornings With the Holy Spirit
Evenings With the Holy Spirit
Revival Hubs Rising
The Next Great Move of God
Developing Faith for the Working of Miracles Breaking the Miracle Barrier
Decoding the Mysteries of Heaven's War Room Jezebel's Revenge
The Making of a Watchman

You can download Jennifer's mobile apps by searching for "Jennifer LeClaire" in your app store and find Jennifer's podcasts on iTunes.

GET IGNITED! JOIN THE IGNITE NETWORK

I believe in prophetic ministry with every fiber of my being, but we all know the prophetic movement has seen its successes and failures. With an end times army of prophets and prophetic people rising up according to Joel 2:28 and Acts 2:17-20, it's more important than ever that we equip the saints for the work of prophetic ministry. Enter Ignite.

Ignite is a prophetic network birthed out of an encounter with the Lord that set a fire in my hearts to raise up a generation of prophets and prophetic people who flow accurately, operate in integrity, and pursue God passionately. I am laboring to cultivate a family of apostolic and prophetic voices and companies of prophets in the nations who can edify, comfort and exhort each other as we contend for pure fire in the next great move of God. My vision for Ignite covers the spiritual, educational, relational and accountability needs of five-fold ministers and intercessory prayer leaders. You can learn more at www.ignitenow.org.

AWAKENING PRAYER HUBS

The Awakening Prayer Hubs mission in any city is to draw a diverse group of intercessors who have one thing in common: to contend for the Lord's will in its city, state and nation.

The vision of Awakening Prayer Hubs is to unite intercessors in cities across the nations of the earth to cooperate with the Spirit of God to see the second half of 2 Chronicles 7:14 come to pass: "If My people, who are called by My name, will humble themselves and pray, and seek My face and turn from their wicked ways, then I will hear from heaven, and will forgive their sin and will heal their land."

For many years, intercessors have been repenting, praying, and seeking God for strategies. Awakening Prayer Hubs intercessors will press into see the land healed, souls saved, churches established, ministries launched, and other Spirit-driven initiatives. Awakening Prayer Hubs intercessors will help undergird other ministries in their city, partnering with them in prayer where intercession may be lacking. Although Awakening Prayer Hubs are not being planted to birth churches, it is possible that churches could spring up from these intercessory prayer cells if the Lord wills.

You can find out more about this prayer movement at www.awakeningprayerhubs.

You can also join the Awakening House Church Movement at awakeninghousechurch.com or plant a house of prayer via Awakening House of Prayer.